Diasporic indian women writers

Quest for Identity in Their Short Stories

Diasporic indian women writers

Quest for Identity in Their Short Stories

Telugu Sireesha

Prestige

an international publishing house

Published by
Prestige Books
3/28, East Patel Nagar
New Delhi 110 008
Ph. 9818755529
email: prestigebooks@gmail.com
website: asiabookclub.com

Associate Office
60/29-45 Parramatta Road,
Concord, NSW 2137
Australia

ISBN: 81-7851-056-1

Printed at Chaman Offset Press, New Delhi 110 002

Contents

for

my parents

and

in loving memory of

my Chinnanna

Acknowledgements

I express my immense gratitude to innumerable people who helped and supported me all through the period of my book, with their comments, suggestions and most importantly by providing me relief with their presence. I thank one and all.

I thank Presitge Books, New Delhi for publishing my book and a special thanks to Dr. Dhawan who motivated me in this respect. Dr. Suman Bala, University of Delhi, gave some invaluable suggestions as a meticulous editor.

I thank the University of Hyderabad and all the teachers of the Department of English with whom I spent many wonderful years and formed an emotional bond. Of all the people, I would like to thank Prof. Alladi Uma for being there for me. This project happened just because of you ma'am. Special thanks to Prof. Sridhar, Dr. Suneetha Rani, Prof. Raghuram Raju, Prof. Mohan Ramanan and Prof. Sachidananda Mohanty. I am also grateful to the Centre for "Indian Diaspora" and Prof. Chandra Sekhar Bhatt especially, for taking me into the "limelight," to the world of "diaspora."

This is the apt time for me to thank the Vanguri Foundation in Houston that sponsored my stay in the United States of America. I thank the special person behind this venture, Dr. Chitten Raj who made my dreams come true. I am grateful to all the families who provided hospitality during my stay in the United States with their love and warmth, putting up with any inconvenience that may have been caused while accommodating me in their houses.

My sincere gratitude to Mr. Indraganti Srikantha Sarma and Indraganti Janaki Bala; Florence, Praveen, Jo, Radhi, Sriram,

Tanuja, Sridevi, Srikanth, Sandhya, Maha, Praveen, Vamshika, Kishore, cigar Srinivas, for being there with me as a beam of support to lean on; to all my friends in the United States of America, Chandra, Renu, Sunil, Jyoti, Vamsi, Sandhya, Chalapathi, Anupama, Neha, Ajay, Swati, Vijay, Tripura who encouraged me during this endeavour; to all my family Amamma, Jaathaya, Chinnaana, Auntymummy, Mavayya, Atha, Uncle, Aunty, my Telugu family, Naanamma, Madhu Chinnaana, Vanaja Aunty, Shanti Aunty, Athas and Mamas, and all my cousins for their love, support, patience and encouragement and a warm welcome whenever I visited them. Their unconstrained love is a constant reminder that there is infinitely more to life than we tend to imagine; to Chelli and Richards for caring and loving me sincerely. Dolly, Sushma, Sangeetha, Tinku, Tittu, Prakash, being there for me sharing their love and affection. I could not have asked for better sibling and cousins. Thank you all for loving me and supporting me. I love you all so much. My deepest love to the most cute, adorable kid on this earth, my sweet little Jessica.

Special thanks to my parents-in-law, brothers, sisters-in-law, brother in-law and lovable little kids.

To Sridhar, for being my *Life*.

I am sincerely obliged to my Mom and Dad for their love, patience, understanding and support. Daddy, Mummy you always believed in me in each phase of my life and provided me everything that I have asked for. You have not only given me life but also made it worth living. Thank you very much for your prayers. I love you.

Last but not the least, to God whom I trust, for His infinite mercy upon me. All my praises belong to You alone. This is what helped me pull through difficult times. Without Your love and blessings, this would have remained a dream.

Chapter 1

Introduction

The word "diaspora" derives from the Greek "dia" (through) and "sperien" (to scatter). According to Webster's dictionary, diaspora refers to "dispersion", and so the word embodies a notion of a centre, a 'home' from where the dispersion occurs. It invokes images of multiple journeys. The dictionary in addition highlights the word's association with the dispersion of Jews after the Babylonian exile. We have both the meanings—as a spread of population and a forcible dispersal. Diaspora does not have nomadic existence in that though it suggests a movement from one place to another, and then, perhaps, yet another it always carries the memory of the original homeland.

At the heart of the notion of diaspora is the image of a journey. Yet not every journey can be understood as that of a diaspora. Diasporas are clearly not the same as casual travel. Nor do they refer to temporary sojourns. Paradoxically, diasporic journeys are essentially about settling down, about having roots elsewhere. The concept of diaspora means different things to different people at different points of time, place and circumstance. Today the meaning of diaspora could be limited to any sizeable community of a particular nation outside its own country, sharing some common bonds that give the community a consequent identity.

Diaspora is not a metaphor for individual exile. Rather, it emerges out of migration of people, whether they travel collectively or as individuals or as households or in various other combinations. Diaspora is a place of long-term, if not permanent, community formation. According to me, the word diaspora often invokes the imagery of traumas of separation and dislocation, and this is certainly a very important aspect of the migratory experience. But diaspora is also understood as a site of hope, of new beginnings.

People have been migrating since evolution, in search of better living. The process of migration is a continuous one, whether it is within a nation or across nations. The migrants not only take their skill and expertise, but also their culture, modes of life and ideologies to their destination. They migrate as manual workers, highly qualified specialists, entrepreneurs, family members of previous migrants and so on. Migration develops, links areas of origin and destination and can change demographic, economic and social structures to create a new cultural identity. It is in this context of formation of communities away from their motherland that the word, diaspora finds a place in literature.

The experience of voluntary migration is very different. You choose to go to a different place and then you start saying you are a diaspora and you have lost your homeland. I am talking of the experience of people of one country going to another for any of the various reasons I have mentioned earlier. In the Indian context, basically it is a case of separation. According to Kapil Kapoor, in his keynote address "Theorizing Diaspora and the Indian Experience" in Sushma J. Varma and Radhika Seshan's *Fractured Identity*, diaspora is like a "leaf falling off a tree, the leaf separates from the tree and it's wafted away, far away" (35-36). Like the leaf separating from a tree, a person is wrenched away from where s/he has belonged for years. The reason for quoting this is, when we converse about diasporic experience, it is the experience of the individual who undergoes separation. I say more of the individual experience because literature deals with a specific individual, a specific time and a specific situation.

Indian immigrants form a large chunk of diaspora all over the world. Moreover, the job market that has opened up as a result of globalization has made the potential of Indians more visible. Along with the market exchange, there has also been a social and cultural exchange. It is in this context, that the literature emerging from the diasporic people assumes significance. The literature of the Indian diaspora is that body of writing produced in English by people who identify themselves as being of Indian heritage living outside their own land. According to Sushma J. Varma and Radhika Seshan in *Fractured Identity*, diasporic studies are only about two decades old, for such studies mainly began in the 1980s, with increased globalization. Though Indian diasporic literature has been in the limelight for some time now, it is in the past twenty years or so, that it has been recognized as a body of literature, a distinct stream of literature that wants to be identified as "Indian" as well as "global."

To me the story of Indian diaspora is one of sweat and toil often washed with tears, of achievements despite impediments, of educational advancement and economic progress, of political success at times etc. With these implications, the diasporic community has also inevitably produced works of literature illustrative of their history and heritage, of their own awareness of the society and its problems, its achievements, its limitations and frustrations among others.

If you go to any University in the United States and look at what they mean by "Courses in Indian Literature", 80% of the texts are from diasporic literature. Therefore the diaspora has become a substitute for the homeland. In what follows, we shall outline a catalogue of important themes and issues that can be pursued in the study of Indian diaspora through the writings of Indian diasporic writers in America. It must be noted that the questions and ideas raised by these themes and issues can best be done through a multidisciplinary approach.

In order to understand diasporic identity the concept of diaspora is approached as a theme in literary representations, while probing into displacement and cultural dislocation. Diasporic people as individuals with different identities continuously search for their homes they have left behind. The diasporic experience as reflected in literature not only includes issues of identity and alienation that are often talked about but also the aspect of community formation in a new land based on similar language and regional backgrounds.

Most of the Indian diasporic literature that I am acquainted with depicts the experiences of Indians in a foreign land. While each writer has a different story to narrate, there definitely emerge certain common themes. The enigma of arrival in an alien land and culture, getting reconciled, getting accepted and finally the dilemma that exists in balancing two different worlds often figure in diasporic writing one way or the other. Issues concerning the diaspora would also include questions of culture and multiculturalism.

The category called "Indian diaspora" has been used in academic discourse. Much, almost all of the diasporic literature that gets published and gets attention is written in English. Literature in Indian languages written by diasporic people is often neglected. Generally speaking, Asian Indian literature in English is prominently featured across the world both in the academy and on the internet, but literature in Indian languages, especially Telugu, has not received its due recognition. In spite of want of recognition, there are a fair number of writers from India who write in their languages and Telugu is no exception. South Asian diaspora is strewn with the names of Indian writers, from V.S. Naipaul to Bharati Mukherjee, and to the more recent Jhumpa Lahiri but Telugu names are hard to find.

When the identity of Hindi is equated with the Indian national identity, the identity of Telugu demands that it is different, and both national and legitimate. My study identifies diaspora in linguistic and cultural terms. Language is an important vehicle for maintaining ethnic identity. It is an ethnic symbol, which distinguishes one group of diaspora from the other. The study of the Indian diaspora in America interests me for it opens up several themes and raises many issues which have relevance to an understanding of the multicultural experience both from the point of view of America and that of the diasporic Indians there.

Such a study is also important for the western people, as it would shed some light on the nature and dynamics of Indian society and culture. This whole idea needs a linguistic approach but my constraints have limited my interest in perceiving culture through language in a literary perspective. The linguistic approach would strengthen my book but the fear of taking too many approaches stopped me from that. I looked at language as literature and not in lingual terms.

I have specifically chosen Telugus in America for the interviewees affirmed that the largest number of Telugu immigrants reside in the United States. Through generations, Telugu people in different lanαs like Malaysia, Fiji, South Africa, etc., have been writing in Telugu but their literature has not been preserved. Thus, the experiences of these Telugu people and their way of living in these lands are unknown to us. But for the past three decades Telugu people who migrated to the United States have been writing in Telugu which we now read as diasporic Telugu literature. The relation between the Telugus in America and their counterparts living around the world as well as relatives back home is not only a matter of memories, but it has been an ongoing and continuous relationship. These transnational relations can be broadly divided into two categories, i.e. 'micro' and 'macro' relations.

'Micro' level relations are more adapted and informal in nature. Telugus continue to keep in touch with friends and relatives back home and in other countries all over the world. These personal links are maintained through telephone calls, letters, internet and personal visits. The 'macro-level' transnational networks among the Telugus can be analysed from two perspectives. First, the networks between the Telugus in the United States and with their relatives back home, and secondly, the networks between Telugus living all over the world. In contrast to the ex-indentured immigrants, Telugu immigrants in the contemporary period have been able to maintain close ties both at social and economic levels. These ties get manifested in the form of literary works written by these people. The issues they are concerned with are portrayed and reflected in these fictional works.

This book is an attempt to understand the methods of adaptation and acquisition of cultural competence by women writers in the diaspora, as viewed by themselves, and the impact of bi-cultural situations on their lives and attitudes. It intends to explore literature written in Telugu and in English by women writers. The reason for confining this study to women writers is that, in general, women living in the American diaspora have not publicly expressed their feelings of dislocation caused by immigration. So it has become difficult to have access to their lives personally but their unrevealed ideas were reflected in their writings. As such their writings are distinct, specific, complex in their own way, and different from male writers.

A woman writing thinks back through her mother's experience bringing in an emotional envisioning. This envisioning creates a different perspective, a question rather than an answer. This question is addressed both to the individuals and their writings:

> Therefore God created Eve from man. And Adam said, this is now bone of my bones, and flesh of my flesh: she shall be called Woman, because she was taken out of man. (*The Holy Bible*, Gen: 2-28, 29)

I use this quote from my personal perspective of being a Christian woman. According to the Holy Bible, woman was generated out of man, depicting man as the most supreme power. This notion of man's supremacy has continued for generations even in the writings of the Hindu women though they talk of woman's power as "adi shakti."

Most of the writings of Indian diasporic women attempt neither to fight male domination nor to compromise themselves. But they portray the reality of what we call "femaleness"— marriage, sex, children, culture and the socially acceptable position of being a woman. It is not only the present era but the creation alone concedes man to be the superior person in the family and his wife to be his subordinate.

With more and more writers of Indian origin settling abroad and engaging themselves in creative writing in the countries of their domicile, the theoretical problem arises in the critical parameters by which their works have to be judged. Research-based studies[1] in literature indicate that varying styles are used in the literature of the diaspora and they often have an impact on migrant's status in host country with focus or linkage to Indian culture.

As comparative and interdisciplinary research is most useful to study the diaspora, I do so through an exploratory study of Indian women writers writing in Telugu and English in the United States. Indian English literature in America has acquired richness by the immigrants who have ably utilized the medium of English for creative expression. Their writings tell us that they have got used to their changed identities and traditions. This does not mean that they have left their homelands. We find their writings forming an emotional bond with their new domicile status. Almost all the diasporic works deal with the concept of cultural transplantation and each migrant has her own story to tell.

Identity depends on the sense of displacement, loss of home, longing to return, culture, ethnic consciousness, religion, caste groups, language, territoriality, etc. As language is used as a marker of identity, Telugu women find it difficult to adopt both the regional identity and the identity of being an Indian. I have discovered various factors in my research, one being the struggle of Indians to promote their own regional language apart from being an "Indian" alone. The diasporic writers writing in Telugu say that they have their own style with which they express their emotions and ideas freely. They say that they do not fear anyone and are not jealous of the fellow writers nor do they expect awards. They do not have the desire to earn money out of their works. They just write to preserve language in this hybrid cultural community. In contrast we see some of the writers writing in English, making a living out of their works.

The diasporic Telugu writers aspire that language and literature should reach the future generations. But writers writing in English are different. They want their literature to reach out to all levels of readers. The Telugu diasporic writers do not seem to be interested in reaching a Telugu audience in India. This group writes for their own immigrant people. They seem to be speaking only to the Telugu readership in the United States. They confess that they themselves are the writers, poets, audience, readers and critics. They write to cherish the past and also the fear of loss makes them want to preserve their language for the coming generations. Their writings cannot be compared to the ones writing back in India as the writers in India cannot be as outspoken in their writings because they fear criticism and they earn a living out of their works.

Here I am not comfortable in discussing about the readership in India because of the lack of material available in India written by Telugu diasporic writers. These writings are not easily accessible to people in India. They are published only in a few journals and magazines like "Rachana" and "Andhra Jyoti" when compared to the works in English written by diasporic writers that have great importance. Books written by Bharati Mukherjee, Jhumpa Lahiri, Chitra Banerjee Divakaruni are prescribed as course texts in academia. As such I have not been able to understand the level of comparison between the two and have not been able to justify it.

Hence we find a difference in their mode of expression and the structure of audience. We find Telugu writers in America write for a private audience with whom they link themselves in their day-to-day lives, whereas Telugu writers in India write for a public audience. The audience is wider in terms of reading, marketing and publication. We find that their works are also less provocative, while dealing with sensitive challenging aspects regarding family and society.

This new world of literary consciousness has given rise to Telugu diasporic literature. This not only preserves language for the diasporic people but also develops relations between countries and continents, thus spreading diasporic experiences. This helps in spreading language to different parts of the world, not just limiting it to a particular part in a country. Diasporic Telugu women writers, in spite of their own intention to write for themselves, make this literature a part of world literature.

Increasingly the terms which are gaining popularity are "expatriate" and "diaspora." The word diaspora as we have already noted literally means a scattering. Further categories emerge through the use of such words as "immigrant", "exile", and "refugee." Their use attempts to give some indication of the ideologies, choices, reasons and compulsions which may have governed the act of migration. While "immigrant" defines a location, a physical movement, "exile" indicates a compulsory isolation. In the Indian context perhaps all meanings are true with the migratory movements having been governed by different reasons at different times but for literary people it is different.

Now-a-days, many writers use "expatriation" and "immigration" as synonyms. However, it is important to draw a line of demarcation between the two, though that line is a thin one. As the term implies, expatriation focuses on the native land that has been left behind, while immigration denotes the country into which one has ventured as an immigrant. In other words, the expatriate lives on her/his "ex" status while the immigrant celebrates her/his present status in the new country. My interest lies in the stories that deal with the "immigrant" status of diasporic origin.

There are different aspects of diasporic Telugu literature and varied methods used in it. I have differentiated diasporic literature produced in America into three different types:

1. Few literary works and lyrical poetry are written using the method of the ancient grammatical linguistic approach that is followed in India.
2. Several stories and poems follow the mode of contemporary Telugu literature.
3. A number of works give significance only to the experiences and themes of immigrant lives in an alien land.

For the communities living in the new world order, the homeland becomes at once remote due to physical distance and yet accessible, with electronic and satellite communication. In these circumstances, the creative writers are distinctly different from what they write about and there is more of imagery than direct experience, especially when dealing with Indian themes. Thus, many of them write mostly about the subsistent experiences in the United States. Therefore, I give importance only to such unique writings of the existent happenings of the immigrants which I term as diasporic literature. The writings of the first two kinds can be written anywhere in the world. Unless the authors disclose their personal details, the reader cannot gauge the authors' place of existence, their relation with society, etc. These immigrants can be put together as expatriates who stay away from their motherland and still cling on to the past culture and tradition, expressing them in their works.

Since being diasporic is a matter of personal choice, at least in the initial years, the journey through life becomes an exploration of alternative modes of adjustment. The possibilities are as diverse and varied, as there are individuals. There is, or can be, no single rule or combination of rules to guide them. Hence, the opinion of the women writers of the diaspora is an invaluable source of information to understand the complexities of the process. Their efforts at a personal level and their perceptions are seen through the financial status of the characters in the short stories.

There is a need to realize the significance of the cultural encounter which takes place in diasporic writing, the bi-cultural pulls and the creation of a new culture which finally emerges. It is important to understand the dynamics of reception from both perspectives as it is rooted in cultural contexts. This sheds light both on the meaning of this writing and on the non-diasporic writing and formation of culture. Reviewing and critiquing diasporic writing is part of my work, for it relates and reflects their experiences and writings.

The high quality of Indian creative writing has been acknowledged by the world's most demanding critics for almost a century now, and there are a few readers of English literature who are unfamiliar with the names and best works of such writers as R.K. Narayan, Raja Rao and so on. But these writers represent a vanishing era and they have been replaced by a new tradition, where many of them write about the Indian diaspora and its themes. Although many writers of this sort can be taken up for study, I wish to concentrate on a few of them such as Bharati Mukherjee, Chitra Banerjee Divakaruni, Ameena Meer, Hema Nair, and few more writing in English and Yarlagadda Kimeera, Puccha Annapurna, Pudipedhi Seshu Sarma, Radhika Nori, Kanaka Durga, Soma Sudeshana Reddy, Bhagavathi and some others writing in Telugu.

The writers that I am referring to are contemporary authors who have left the Indian sub-continent to live in America sometimes out of choice (to work or to study), and at other times they or their families are required to leave the Indian sub-continent for economic or political reasons. There are commonalities as well as basic differences between each one of the women writers in the way that they relate to the country of their origin and to their immigrant status, thus bringing out the similar and the diverse perceptions and experiences of living in the diaspora.

There are different elements that separate the attitudes of one writer from the other. One is that of the exile of those who have nostalgia for the home country and whose attitude to the host country is negative. The other type behaves as having adapted itself to the western impact. Bharati Mukherjee wants to be a perfect immigrant and she says she is transforming herself. This is reflected in many of her short stories. In her story "Father" in *Darkness*, Mr. Bhowmick is pictured as a man clinging to the ex-status of his life in India. He is seen as an expatriate. He is both a failure in his marital relationship and in his position as a father: "The women in his family were smarter than him. They were cheerful, outgoing, more American somehow" (Mukherjee, "Father" 61).

We see the characters of his wife and daughter as transformed ones. They are more Americanized, and this does not mean that they have left their homeland. They are the examples of those who are not affected by the host country. They retain their own native culture intact with pride. Bharati Mukherjee's works emphasize stories that claim America; they feature subjects who liberate themselves through struggles against racism to a stable identity and location. Moreover, this happens in relation to gender, as Indian women writers attempt to challenge the patriarchal structures from within and portray themselves to the audience as being more subjective and powerful compared to men. Hence we notice that most of the short stories written by these diasporic women writers picture women as protagonists. Mukherjee tends to say that immigration is always a rebirth, a new start of life, a disjuncture of subjectivity.

Runu in "Ultra Sound" in Chitra Banerjee Divakaruni's *Arranged Marriage* finds life in America and its amenities more useful and better than the one in India. During Runu's labour she feels happy staying in America although she desires to go back to India. Having her husband next to her while giving birth to their child binds her in staying back:

> Though Runu looks forward to going back to her mother's house for the delivery, as is the custom, and laments the fact that I can't, I'm not unhappy. In India they don't let husbands into the labor room. And I know that I'll need Sunil with me, holding my hand. (Divakaruni, "Ultra Sound" 214)

Diasporic Indians do not merely have dark experiences but also possess bright ones. Advantages and disadvantages are two sides of the same coin, which cannot be separated. Darkness is followed by light. Similarly, the diasporic people not only face assimilation problems but they also face bright things, which are illustrated in the works of diasporic women writers. The numerous novels, short stories, poems and plays published by the women writers provide not merely a bird's view of life in the diaspora but also the different shades of experiences and responses of different individuals to different situations.

As creative writers, all of them take the familiar and the known, as the basic theme of their literary work, to embellish it by their imagination into works of art. Hence, the themes deal with fictional characters from back home or the story of immigrants' lives with their multifarious nuances in the new home or stories that straddle both the countries in time and space or express multiple subjectivities, as experienced by the characters. The themes, the characters and the stories are thus a true reflection of the reality of the diasporic life of the people in the concerned countries.

Chimata Kamala in her short story "America Illaalu" (American Wife) in *America Telugu Katha* describes the status of an immigrant Indian wife and her problems in adjusting to the fast cultured world. Like many immigrant women she feels it difficult to adjust to the new world and new customs and to leave her past behind. She cannot move freely like an American wife nor sit in the house like an Indian wife: "I am like an American wife poised in the seventh heaven unable to completely behave like an Indian home maker nor can I change myself into an American housewife"[2] (Kamala, "America Illaalu" 79). Chimata Kamala visualizes herself in the character, depicting the problems of a married working woman, struggling to cope both at her workplace and her family. She is observed as an "American wife" who portrays in general the problems of an Indian wife through the character in her story.

We have Soma Sudeshana Reddy's short story "Passing Phase" in *Proceedings of Fourth International Telugu Conference*. The author in the story portrays the changing phases in one's life time. At one time of life, the conflicts between the parents and children trouble them. This exists more in the diasporic families with the intrusion of the alien culture: "Sangita is an American girl brought up in an Indian household. All she could relate to was the American life though she had perceived Indian customs and tasted typical Telugu cuisine." (Reddy, "Passing Phase" 130). The story illustrates the changing phase of parent-child relationship in a new world.

An overview of the stories written in Telugu and English indicates that they focus strongly on the alienation of the diasporic Indians who are often characterized by an overwhelming sense of nostalgia. This sense of nostalgia is enhanced as there is no antagonism towards the home society as they have not come to America because of religious or political persecution at home. As compared to the white migrants of the United States of America, the diasporic Indians notice a cultural difference which may lead to a cultural disorientation. Sometimes, they even provide a critique of the western civilization. In the absence of a shared cultural heritage, the differences are sharpened and the home country acquires a romantic glow. One feels insecure and has to fight against the possibility of an identity crisis.

Writers like Chitra Banerjee Divakaruni, Bharati Mukherjee, Kalasapudi Vasundhara, Chimata Kamala, Puccha Annapurna, Nidadhavolu Malathi and many more write about issues like arranged marriage, culture shocks, racial discrimination, identity crisis. Talking about Nidadhavolu Malathi, she is unique when compared to other writers as she writes both in Telugu and English and was a writer writing in India even before her migration to the United States. After her migration, she started translating diasporic Telugu works into English. She has also established a web-site, "www.thulika.net" where the translated works are obtainable so as to reach the western audience. The major aim of her project is to have all kinds of audience, including the international. The web-site helps the second-generation to read and understand the works, as they are able to read only the English version. Here it is to be observed that though Nidadhavolu Malathi has been contributing a lot to Telugu diasporic literature, it is unfortunate that her works are not published in any of the eight volumes of *America Telugu Kathanika* or in *America Telugu Katha*.

Bharati Mukherjee is the only one of its kind who challenges the translucent lives of the immigrant women signified strong in their characters but always very emotional. Her *Wife* personifies Dimple Dasgupta, as a "psychoneurotic" before marriage, and whose problems get aggravated after her migration to the United States of America. She is the lone female protagonist among all the characters in Bharati Mukherjee's works who feels that she suffers a strong sense of insecurity being a woman. Diverse issues are generated in the lives of the characters, especially because they live in an alien culture.

Meena Alexander is another Indian American immigrant writer who writes poetry and fiction. She is passionately involved with issues like immigration, ethnicity, culture, race relations and discloses them in her works. She is dissimilar from the other writers as far as the religious aspect is concerned. She is a Syrian Christian settled in America, thus most of her works do not deal with the issue of Hinduism in a Christian world.

For many writers including Meena Alexander viewing them in an alien background, having to learn and relearn English has had a tangible effect on them to decolonize themselves linguistically. At times, though they wish to tear themselves away from English, they realize its sheer force as a large number of philosophers and writers from various countries and languages were mainly translated into English. Thus, despite their awareness of the colonial pressure, they find themselves bound to English in an organic way, as the chief medium of expression.[3]

The first-generation of immigrants as a diasporic community is evidently different from the second and the subsequent ones. United States now has an entire generation of diasporic Indians born and brought up in the country. Whether it is a question of ethnic identity, emotional orientation to the ancestral land, the response to social institutions and cultural elements taken from India, or socio-political orientation to America, we can expect significant differences between the first and the second generations of diasporic Indians.

For the first generation, diaspora means strong feeling about the country of their origin, and for the second generation, it means ties with the homeland that get gradually replaced by those with the accepted country because the latter does not remain adopted. It becomes their country, yet not quite. The individuals and families who live at the juncture between two cultures can lay claim belonging to both. Yet for reasons of being born into one culture and living in the second, they are marginal people, very different from the norms set by the majority. Marginality leads to the psychological conflicts of a divided self.

The story of the diaspora in different stages is the resolution of this conflict in the lives of individuals, families and generations. With the loss of a sense of security of a known historical past and of a shared geographical space, their need to belong becomes the key issue. Most of their themes relate to younger generation and their struggles, inter-generational relations, complexities of inter-racial relationships, the painful reality of racism and the sense of feeling peripatetic, caught between parents and mainstream culture.

It is argued that a young Indian growing up in America is exposed to two cultures, one at home and the other at school and as a result, the young person experiences stress and identity conflicts. As both the power of the emotional bond, especially between parents and children, and the power of social sanction are important, family remains an area of ambivalence. For Indian women, family support may also become necessary in the struggle against the onslaught of racism.

Almost all the stories written both in Telugu and English project the same issues. Identity problem and racial discrimination that they face, new world, new customs, language problems, Indian degrees that are not useful in America come up at one time or the other in the short stories. There are many trajectories that I would like to take to dealing with the concept of diaspora, the dating system and the conflicts of the marriage system, nostalgia and their long standing hope to get back to India at any point of their lives, day-to-day life experiences, insecurity that reflects in the lives of the immigrants, struggle between the first and the second generation, the fear of losing their language in a foreign land and many more.

The concept of identity is very important for the diasporic people. Indian immigrants speak different languages and have different professions and vocations but what gives them a commonality of identity is the consciousness of their Indian origin, cultural heritage and a deep attachment to India. According to Indian tradition, the families live together and stick together, so that people can help one another.

Thus, the influence of diaspora and that of the land of their origin, their lives, thoughts and creativity of the women writers have been all-pervasive. There are different levels at which they have related to them. In their personal and professional lives, they have had to make innumerable adjustments in terms of alienation, racism and changing value systems. As minority writers, they have confronted difficulties to establish their identity as women and that too, as South Asian women of Indian origin, in a white, male-dominated society. Most of the writers fall into this pattern. However, Bharati Mukherjee is a bit different from the others as the emphasis in her work is more on the American setting in which the immigrant characters live. While her characters face all the brutalities of the atmosphere around them, they finally emerge as survivors and her mode of bold transformation widened my curiosity.

One aspect that troubles me is her usage of sexual element in many of her stories. The first part generally deals with the settling of the immigrants in a new land and then ends up with the protagonist making love to the person from the American soil. The characters in the stories feel that sex is normal, which, to me, is unrealistic in the writings of most Indian women writers. The stories ultimately show a fascinating picture of modern America and the immigrants' experiences. The story that starts up with many problems and complexities suddenly winds up with love making which is reflexive and unrealistic. It has been challenging for me to compare Bharati Mukherjee with other diasporic women writers.

It is interesting to note the diverse preferences each writer has for acquiring recognition. Diaspora is all about the creation of new identities, space for growth, resolution of conflicts and a new culture, either composite or plural. This is what these creative women writers of Indian origin, living in America, are concerned with and are in the process of accomplishing, each in her own way. The writers have put to use their direct experience of living in the diaspora. Being women, they have done this with great sensitivity, to express through their writing the various gradations in the lives of immigrants of all ages, sexes and generations.

I have gone through a wide range of journals and texts both primary and secondary. The most important primary text is *Contours of the Heart* edited by Sunaina Maira and Rajini Srikanth, a collection of short stories, poems, articles, and essays written in English by diasporic women writers. This book deals with the personal experience of the writers in an alien land. It is a bit different from the other diasporic stories that I have read. The stories are a bit complicated and difficult to understand at first reading. The language and style look more western than Indian.

Arranged Marriage, a collection of short stories by Chitra Banerjee Divakaruni, comprises the lives of Indian-born women, leading their new lives in America with their old treasured beliefs and a desire to achieve success in the new world. And in this battle there arise a lot of conflicts. This is her first collection of short stories, focusing on women from India caught between two worlds. The characters are both liberated and trapped by cultural changes, struggling to carve out an identity of their own. Chitra Banerjee Divakaruni deals with a variety of issues in her book including racism, interracial relations, economic disparity, abortion and divorce. She says that the stories are inspired by her imagination and the experience of others. Her writing often centres on the lives of immigrant women.

The Middleman and Other Stories by Bharati Mukherjee portrays a complete change in the majority of immigrant protagonists in these stories. They are seen as immigrants who have fully adapted themselves to American culture. The immigrants chosen as protagonists in these stories are from Italy, India, Hungary, Vietnam, Afghanistan etc. The author talks about the immigrant experience on the whole and not just from India. She talks about the immigrants from different parts of the world facing a unique problem, "Americanization." *Darkness* is another book by Bharati Mukherjee which is in a sense different from her other works. Love, desire, and romance as experienced by the immigrant men and women from the Indian sub-continent in the new world appear as recurring themes in this collection.

America Telugu Katha edited by Indraganti Srikantha Sarma and Indraganti Janaki Bala is an exclusive collection of short stories written in Telugu by both men and women. The background from which these authors come is also different. Most of the Telugu writers are first-generation immigrants. This generation gap reflects in their writing in the form of conflicts between the first and the second generations. There are eight volumes of *America Telugu Kathanika* edited by Pemmaraju Venugopalarao and the short stories are written in Telugu by men and women in the United States of America. The short stories portray reminiscences of their motherland and the question of language. They are also seen as immigrants searching for their identity that hangs between two worlds. Apart from this, there are various short stories that appeared in different journals, magazines and web-sites.

As stated earlier, these Telugu women writers are writing for themselves, and for their own immigrant people and it has not reached the people who belong to the place of their origin. There are many examples to prove this argument, one such being the absence of Telugu diasporic works in India. When there are tons of writings produced by the people of diasporic origin, why are they not available in India? It is ironic to see that eight volumes of *America Telugu Kathanika* are not easily accessible in India. This lack of material made me travel to the United States of America to meet the writers and gather the material. I have selected a few writers to compare and contrast them with writers writing in English.

These texts are especially valuable since these books give a direct insight into the lives and feelings of women in the diaspora and the issues that they have to face as immigrants, which would otherwise have gone unrecorded. Almost all issues of relevance, i.e., inter-generational/gender conflicts, marital discords and cultural dislocations have been dealt with in their writings. I discuss some of the issues that have been mentioned above in the following chapters. Many of them hinge on the issue of identity and gender. The assertion of identity, and the context of that assertion, is something that is apparently of concern to literary writers and social scientists.

Having set the stage for the exploration of diasporic Indian women writers and their writings in this chapter, I move on to three other chapters in the book. The present chapter forms the introduction to the study which has glanced at some of the theories of diaspora and diasporic literature. It has included the objectives of this study and the relevance of the study of diasporic literature in the present scenario.

Chapter 2 undertakes a critical assessment of the concept of marital relationships and with the identity of the woman playing the character of a lover/wife. Chapter 3 deals with conflicts of the first and second generations. In studying how Indian values are translated from one generation to the next, an essential variable for examination becomes the parent-child relationship. This is what I deal with in my third chapter. Chapter 4 provides various aspects that revolve around diasporic literature with reference to the selected texts. This includes the identity of the woman vis-à-vis culture and religion, and her identity at her workplace. The concluding chapter summarizes all the sections and the findings of my book. This is followed by a bibliography.

Finally, I would like to say that the writers of both fiction and criticism infuse their writings with emotions of longing and nostalgia, just as they speak of confusion and trauma particularly arising out of displacement. There is a need to establish a connection with others who have similar experiences. They seek communities and individuals with whom they can share their experiences and feel comfortable, though they retain their differences. The community is created. The diaspora is born.

NOTES

1. Two significant studies in this direction are by Kurian and Srivastava, and by Jain.
2. All translations from Telugu are my own.
3. For a discussion of this aspect see Dhawan.

Chapter 2

Family Matters?: Interpersonal Relationships

In this fast growing society, people of different nations, including Indians are migrating to the United States seeking better economic conditions. Today Indians belong to one of the fastest growing ethnic minority groups in the United States of America. As these immigrants are progressively exposed to the standards, norms, and values of western society, the result is an increasing confusion regarding assimilation and acculturation. Indians arrive in societies that are not conducive to their traditional upbringing and are forced to make adjustments to an alien environment. They find it difficult to keep pace with the changes, especially in inter-generational contacts, interpersonal relationships and inter-cultural transformations.

The Indian immigrants find themselves displaced from their roots. They shed their monolithic, national and region-specific identities and become a part of a dual and/or multiple identities. Their position as outsiders in the country of their adoption leads them to create a distinct space. Indian women writers writing away from their motherland have often been caught between these divergent value systems. Many issues are taken up in their stories, the most important one being marriage, which binds families together and helps maintain traditional customs. When a marriage is arranged, it is seen as a union between two families and not of two individuals, as it is in the western world. It is clear that education, religion, national/regional origin and financial security are considered important in addition to physical characteristics.

Most of the stories prove that the diasporic Indian women writers are not different from the women writers back in India though they are placed in a different atmosphere in a different tradition. They have the same notion of paying respect and being obliged to their husbands. But there are some stories which prove that Indian women are neither unpleasant nor tolerant towards their husbands. Both women writers in Telugu and English try to justify these statements through their characters in the short stories.

It has been observed by many authors that Indian immigrants generally maintain their respect for and faith in the Indian value systems and institutions, even though they are critical of India in many ways. For example, they talk about poverty, the population explosion, the caste system and the lack of opportunity for professional advancement in India. However, there seldom is a debate of the basic value system, which develops major social institutions such as marriage and the family. Almost all the writers I discuss come from a Hindu background. So I use the term Indian as interchangeable with Hindu. Based on Hindu scriptures, the marriage system in India was well established in the Vedic period. India is complex and its people are so different in terms of language, caste, customs and beliefs that it is difficult to make generalizations about family life.

During some of the interviews, the respondents emphasized on the point that the Asian Indians place a high value on the family. They say that marriage is a means of maintaining regional, caste and family identity. Marriage is not just between two individuals but rather the blending of two families. Generally, in India, love between husband and wife was supposed to be the result of marriage, rather than a prelude to it. But when we compare it with the marriage system in America, it is quite different. In American society, love and marriage are usually interrelated and the individual has freedom of choice in seeking a partner.

The attitude of Indian immigrants towards love and marriage is quite the opposite to that of Americans.

With this outlook, the book makes a detailed study of some of the literary works written by women writers of the Indian diaspora in America writing in Telugu and English. Yarlagadda Kimeera has written several short stories and is one of the first women writers of North America writing in Telugu. She lives in Silver Spring, Maryland with her family. "Veedina Needalu" (Vanished Shadows) from *America Telugu Katha* is a story of two persons brought up in two different customs. Gopal from India is married to Vandana, an American born Indian, and migrates to the United States. He expects Vandana to be an idiosyncratic Indian wife in every facet including her mental and physical stance. Like most of the Indian men, he tries to be the domineering figure directing his wife in every move, which turns to be a discontent to her. On the contrary, Vandana, born and brought up in America, could not measure up to his expectations:

> Although I told you many times, you don't care for my words. You don't respect me as a husband. How many times did I tell you not to wear such clothes? You know that I hate you calling me 'honey', but you still do so. If this doesn't show your carelessness, then what is it? Dressed up like a prostitute. Shame. It's my ill-fate that I found you. (Kimeera, "Veedina Needalu" 215)

According to the conventional norms, the husband is supposed to be the authoritarian person, whose "impulse" is to take over the family. The wife is his subordinate and is expected to regard him as her master and serve him faithfully. But in this story, we find the opposite.

Indians living abroad generally try to be smarter than the natives of that country, although they forget that in basic emotions there is hardly any difference between the East and the West. The author tries to say that family institution continues to be the core of Indian society and has not experienced a general disintegration. In spite of all the recent changes in the traditional roles and status of women, marriage and family continue to be very significant and meaningful institutions in a woman's life. Though structural changes are taking place in women's roles and marriages, and though new trends are appearing, progress remains slow. Husbands generally wish to remain the authority figures and decision makers in many cases, like Gopal in "Veedina Needalu." It is a different and well-laid story of a couple from diverse backgrounds caught up in a stifling relationship in the global capital, America.

This concept of characters with mixed backgrounds is portrayed in Chitra Banerjee Divakaruni's short story "Doors" in *Arranged Marriage*. Preeti from India migrates to the United States during her childhood. She marries Deepak, her friend from the University. Her mother warns her to be careful with Deepak because she personifies herself as an immigrant wife who endures in transforming her life. And she is cynical if her daughter can go through the adjustments in the traditional married life of an Indian:

> "It's never too late to stop yourself from ruining your life," her mother said. "What do you really know about how Indian men think? About what they expect from their women?" (Divakaruni, "Doors" 184)

Even Deepak's friends tease him during his marriage with Preeti, by simplifying the gesticulations of all Indian women in America.

> "'American' women are always bossing you, always thinking about themselves. . . ."
>
> "It's no wonder we call them ABCDs—American-Born-Confused-*Desis*," quipped another friend. (Divakaruni, "Doors" 185)

This gives us a clear picture of the perplexed feelings of Indian men about immigrant women. Here we see both the mother and friends censorious concerning the marriage of Preeti and Deepak. Chitra Banerjee Divakaruni constructs the story in a unique method to support her argument.

Indian men wish to marry Indian women as they believe that they would be more submissive than American women because of their background and cultural setting, as such they have an approach to consider that only Indian women can occupy certain sanctified spaces. Such spaces are disregarded for they bring along with them standards and expectations that spiritually and emotionally confine Indian women, with very little room for adjustment. Preeti and Deepak's marital life runs smoothly with mutual love and respect, breaching the hasty views of their friends. Very soon, the friends are glad to notice the blissful marital life of Preeti and Deepak.

> And of course I know how stubborn and close mouthed *you* are: But I think you've both adjusted wonderfully. At the risk of sounding clichéd, I'd say you're a perfectly matched couple! (Divakaruni, "Doors" 187)

But misfortune ruins their relationship in the form of Deepak's childhood friend, Raj who arrives from India to do his masters in America. He stays in Deepak's house and Preeti does not appreciate their intimacy and develops a sense of envious sensitivity against Raj.

> "Well, as a matter of fact I was thinking of taking a couple days off. You know—take Raju to San Francisco may be down to Carmel." Preeti was surprised by the sudden surge of jealousy she felt. (Divakaruni, "Doors" 191)

Preeti brought up in America was unaware of the degrees of intimacy and affection of Indian people of the same sex, and she could not tolerate the relationship between Deepak and Raj. Though an Indian, she is confused by the two traditions and cultures, one she is born into and the other she has adapted to. Thus both the stories "Veedina Needalu" (Vanished Shadows) and "Doors" prove that American society has had an impact on the way one views marital relationships. They find themselves half-way between the continuity of the traditional Indian values and the influence of 'progressive' American ones. The concept of chastity haunts them like a ghost at noon. They cannot be completely westernized in their thoughts and feelings.

Vandana born in America forgets the tradition of an Indian family which is usually defined as patriarchal and authoritarian and tries to be dictatorial to her husband, resulting in the failure of her relationship. Preeti spoils her marital life with her impulsiveness and messes up the responsibility of being an understanding wife and a good host. "Doors" is an ironic title for the story. Preeti is depicted by the author who is always observed closing the doors behind her. The author uses the title as an image of her protagonist shutting out the emotions and attachments deep inside her. We can say that Preeti is not only found closing the doors of the room but also closing the doors of her heart against the marital relationship with Deepak.

Puccha Annapurna, postgraduate in English literature, has written many short stories and poems in America. "Pelli" (Marriage) from *America Telugu Katha* epitomizes an Indian couple in the United States, the protagonist Sridevi of forty-nine years and her husband Bhargav of fifty-seven going through a vital phase at their age. The author begins and ends the story with neat arguments and conclusions in the conversations between Sridevi and Bhargav. They even comment on issues of a married man remarrying in his middle age; comparing their relationships, they are glad they are not affected by such a culture and that there is no drastic change. Going through their discussions, we realize that Sridevi is happy enough that their generation was not influenced much with the American impact.

But towards the end, she is shocked to hear her husband's decision of remarrying a cousin of his. She tries to persuade her husband but fails in changing her husband's decision and like a conventional Indian wife feels her husband's happiness as hers and accepts his decision. Though she has to share her husband in her middle age, she accepts his desire in order to retain her own marital relationship. In the beginning, Sridevi, who argues on silly matters like distracting relationships, transforms towards the end, approving his relationship like a typical Indian woman who is very much committed to the institution of marriage.

The author tries to give a clear description of the story through various images. She talks about a cross with lights shimmering by the device of electrical energy:

> Though it is not easy to shine like these artificial lights, she spent a few moments looking at that symbol of faith which was trying to maintain its existence in the unnatural light. (Annapurna, "Pelli" 106)

This portrays the image of an Indian wife who surrenders to the environment she stays in. It is not only the cross that is gleaming with artificial power but also the protagonist. Sridevi is pictured as an immigrant woman trying to endure and be content in the mechanical world, not by the glare of fantasy land but by the Indian customs and traditions that had taught her to face any situation with an optimistic look. For many Indian wives, the road to marriage was not one that led towards personal fulfillment. Rather, it was a vocation that called for self-surrender, self-sacrifice and physical and emotional distance.

Age factor is also important in the story as both the characters in their middle age have to undergo the pressure of new transformations. The American ambience also plays an essential role on Bhargav's decision of re-marrying in his age, for according to the western culture, age is not a chief factor for marriage. In contrast, the Indian traditional norms say that the husband should not re-marry till the death of his wife and the same practice pertains to the wife. If they were in India, the system of marriage might not have supported him in his decision. And also the pressure of the society would not have allowed him to take a serious step as marrying at the age of fifty-seven. Polygamy, namely having two wives at the same time, is illegal in United States too. But the marriage system of America is different from the Indian marriage system.

While the Hindu marriage is the keystone to all family patterns that have characterized and shaped Indian society, the American concept of marriage is quite different. The ideal Indian family believes in marriage as a sacred and social duty, and a family responsibility, and stresses the importance of marital relationship. On the other hand, the Americans view marriage as an agreement, the married couple as a decision-making unit without any involvement or interference by relations. Thus, it is clear that there arise certain conflicts between the two systems for the immigrants.

Even though many changes take place in the psyche of Indians after immigration, some remain the same as they were in their homeland. Many changes occur in the psyche of the immigrants. Some of the immigrants remain their old selves. Though some change outwardly, their basic attitude towards the family and marriage does not change. Generally, the commitment of Indians to the institution of marriage remains strong, in many cases because wives adjust to the decisions and attitudes of their husbands in order to sustain the relationship. As such, we see Sridevi as a representative of the traditional image of an Indian wife. And we as readers can easily analyze the mindset of the author, when Sridevi approves the notion of her husband's decision of a second marriage while the wife is living.

The story depicts the unchanged traditions and values of the Indian women altering to every obstacle entering their lives. The impact of the heavy western influence on Indians might have also been one of her reasons to choose this theme for her story. I have come across a dialogue in a diasporic Hindi movie "Hollywood Bollywood" by Deepa Mehta which says, "Sacrifice is the human torch of Indian values," that proved to be true for the protagonist. Wives being devoted to their husbands do not die out even with the changed culture or customs.

Back in India as well we find women writers writing with the similar concept of wives being obedient to their husbands. Rukmani in Kamala Markandaya's *Nectar in a Sieve* never forgets that a woman's place is by her husband's side. Though she comes from a better family than her husband, nothing obstructs her from admiring her husband. She accepts her husband's wishes as hers and works for his benefit. Rukmani's life revolves around her husband like a standard Indian wife.

Pudipedhi Seshu Sarma is another Telugu writer, a doctor by profession. In addition to her vocation, she is an artist, a director, a dancer and a singer. In addition she is a social worker who works for the development of rural areas in Andhra Pradesh, India. Her short story "Agaadham" (Unfathomable) from *America Telugu Kathanika* is a reflection of an immigrant Indian woman who fears the loss of her marital relationship:

> When the kids were young, he was very loving. The compassion and patience he had was enormous. But for the past three to four years he has started getting irritated with me even for little issues. After seeing all this I wonder if he has an aversion towards me, as I never felt this before. (Seshusarma, "Agaadham" 5)

The protagonist in this story has a propensity towards her family in every petite aspect, which results in problematic conditions for her husband. She tries to avert the isolation by taking part in all the decisions at every point and implementing them. The husband does not tolerate the fact of his wife becoming authoritative in the family, and as a result differences crop up between the husband and wife. It is surprising to see that there were never any attempts to sort out the problems that stressed their marital life.

They are involved in their own thoughts giving less importance to the other. The story reflects the alienation and the solitude they face in a foreign land as immigrants. Through this story, the writer tells us that there should be proper understanding between husband and wife, which is lacking in the present days. The hustle and bustle of the fast-paced world of today fails to give people a chance to sit and share their feelings with one another.

Some of the interviews in my field study define marriage as an important element in the life of an individual. They say that compromise in a marriage is very important so that you do not grow apart. Some of them even argue that open communication is important in marriage. One should be able to speak out one's heart and true feelings. Marriage should be more of a friendship. There should be a lot of freedom to speak or just be there for the partner in his/her needs forever. Lack of communication creates a lot of trouble to the partners in many cases, which is reflected in "Agaadham." Thus, towards the end, the wife realizes the mistake and decides to bridge the gap between them:

> To what sort of mental agonies will this lead! No! No use!! I need to open my heart to him. He should understand my sorrow. I should understand his. We should understand each other. For better or worse, by doing something this gap should be filled. (Seshusarma, "Agaadham" 10)

The marriage bond, which is still sacrosanct in India, is gradually breaking down under the pressure of new needs in different backgrounds. One always needs another's touch in an emotional crisis, which is realized by the characters towards the end. And finally all mental doubts and apprehensions that cloud their lives are removed and their marital life is strengthened again.

The alienation in marital life is quite disturbing to both the partners creating an unpleasant atmosphere. "Surprise" by Pudipedhi Seshu Sarma from *America Telugu Kathanika*, replicates the alienation of an Indian woman married to an Indian immigrant in the United States. Latha and Suresh settled in America are observed suffering from lack of emotion in the westernized life of America. Everything seems mechanical to Latha. She avoids all her friends and gatherings. She even disagrees when their friends plan a surprise party to celebrate their twenty-fifth wedding anniversary, but finally she gives in and attends it with Suresh.

After the party, Suresh surprises Latha and his friends with his appointment order as an advisor of "Governor's Task Force and Health Care Reforms." When everyone starts celebrating this occasion, Latha stuns him with her surprise announcement. She unveils her decision of going back to India forever. Latha is portrayed as a woman taking care of her husband and children all through her life and not of her own self. She reveals her disappointment as an Indian wife, failing to be a wife to her husband and a mother to her children:

> Not one of my desires were fulfilled in life. . . . I never liked public life. But it was unavoidable in my life . . . this is all my fate, my luck. But . . . for twenty five years I lived in self-degradation. (Seshu Sarma, "Surprise" 55)

Sociologist Sati S. Dasgupta in the book, *On the Trial of an Uncertain Dream: An Immigrant Experience in America*, says that the women spend most of their time in the company of other women before marriage as well as after marriage. Thus their lives for the most part are spent within their female world. But an Indian immigrant woman after marriage has to leave her family connections and friends to migrate to another world with her husband. She sees the whole world in her male companion. And thus the bonding is lost forever for the Indian immigrant women.

Hence Latha experiences a gap within her family though they were next to her. Everyone in the family is so engaged in his/ her own personal work that none realizes the need to spend time with Latha. She is left unaccompanied all through her marital life and has nothing to do but to take care of her family and home. The seclusion in an alien land frustrates her but at the same time the American atmosphere helps her in taking a strong decision to seek her own happiness rather than struggling for the others. Latha at a crucial point takes a strong step ahead to live a life according to her desire, unlike the traditional Indian woman who regards the husband's happiness as hers. This would have been less possible if she was in India, due to the pull of the conventional customs of marriage and with interference of her kith and kin.

Lalitha Jonnal is a unique writer writing for the past ten years and is a good translator as well. She belongs to a local writers' group and is presently working on two novels which are ready for publication. Her "Abhyaagathudu" (Guest) from *America Telugu Kathanika* is different from the other short stories written by diasporic Indian women in Telugu in the way that it deals with the issues of conjugal relationship. In the previous stories, we have seen the marital relationship as a strained discourse with less attachment between the husband and wife. We have also argued that the mechanical world has changed the emotional link between the partners. But this story is quite the opposite.

Lila and Raghu, a happily married couple in their mid-age live peacefully in their own world sharing love and warmth. At this juncture, a new person enters their life, it is Lila's college day's passion. He expresses his platonic love to Lila and leaves her home with a gift of the works that he had written. Raghu comes to know about this incident and understands their respect towards each other:

> I thought a lot, of his emotions and his affection towards you. Neither of you hurt me . . . or cheated me. His mind and emotions are very tranquil. (Jonnal, "Abhyaagathudu" 89)

This story proves that a proper understanding between the husband and wife can clear away many obstacles that encompass their lives. Raghu and Lila are represented as a couple that has immense trust for each other. This can also be stated as the positive impact of American life on them. The modern thinking of Raghu formulates him to view his marital life in a balanced manner. The narration also proves that apart from the disadvantages, there are also advantages for the immigrants without the interference of the society in their lives. This is an opportunity for both the husband and wife to get to know each other.

In America, generally the relationship functions between two individuals with similar views. The alliance of Raghu and Lila is seen as an interaction of two people with different viewpoints that are brought together by the fundamental unit of human society, the family. The author all through the story presents her arguments well. She is careful not to build the reader to suspect any problem in the relationship between Raghu and Lila. A young writer dealing with middle-aged characters in a well-balanced manner highlights the fact that, being a doctor, she understands the psychology of people.

Kanaka Durga is a freelance writer and has been writing short stories for the past ten years. Most of her stories are published in different magazines and journals. "Henpecked" by Kanaka Durga in *America Telugu Kathanika* portrays two sets of life partners in two different situations. Rajendra and Prerana's married life in the story is a success. They have good communication and share every minute thing with proper understanding and love. Most women prefer to have a relationship of partnership than of inequality. Though they may not mind assuming the subordinate position, women strongly feel that the wife's position should be of a respected subordinate with a personality of her own and of a good companion to the husband:

> Rajendra, Prerana met in a college. . . . Both went for a registered marriage. Both are job holders. All friends met the same way they did before a traditional marriage (Durga, "Henpecked" 95).

The intimacy of Rajendra and Prerana's married life proves that with proper planning, one can lead a happy marital life without any hurdles.

But in contrast Sekhar and Ramya's marital life is a failure. They are portrayed as a miserable couple who fight over every issue that crop up in their lives. This couple is a representative of a typical Indian husband and wife, struggling to adjust to the culture and tradition they have inherited. Sekhar gives importance to society and fears that his friends would tease him if he helps his wife in her domestic work. As a typical Indian husband, he tries to be an authoritarian figure, always ruling over his wife messing up his marital relationship:

> Disputes arose between Ramya and Sekhar for some time. Sekhar did not change his attitude. Irritated, Ramya packed her things to live away from him. (Durga, "Henpecked" 97)

The husband assumes himself to be superior over his wife, thus resulting in a gap in the relationship. Earlier, in families, there was hardly any recognition of individual interests or aspirations of husbands and wives. The wife's only concern was to see that she performed properly all the services needed by her husband, whose satisfaction was her "joy" in life.

As pointed out by many sociologists, women's education and employment have affected their attitudes and actual behaviour with regard to the traditional relationships between spouses. The educated modern woman is no longer willing to accept complete dominance of her husband. Ramya's individuality and self-dependence portrays her as a woman with principles. Her strong-mindedness formulates her husband to realize his mistake, changing him into an understanding and loving companion.

"Chaitanyam" (Awareness) in *America Telugu Kathanika* is a short story by Soma Sudheshna Reddy who represents her central character Madhavi into a transformed woman after her sexual experience on the first night of her marriage. Gopal and Madhavi lead a disturbing marital relationship and as a result Madhavi considers thrown out away from the family and society:

> You are typically old fashioned. You don't change and you will not also. The children also feel awkward when they look at you. So saying Gopalam walked away treading heavily on Madhavi's heart. She mourned day and night. (Reddy, "Chaitanyam" 81)

Sometimes marriage disrupts the interpersonal relationships of the immigrant women, instead of enriching them. The protagonist spends all her time with her family; hence she feels left out and cannot fit into the community around her. This nurtures a sense of loneliness and boredom. Men have contact with the outside world through their jobs, and women mostly stay at home, building a cocoon around them, with the feeling of "not belonging here." When Madhavi tries to search out for happiness through serving her husband and family, Gopal shatters her expectations by divorcing her and going away for a second marriage.

This confrontation between Gopal and Madhavi transforms Madhavi from a timid woman to a bold woman ready to face every hurdle in her life in a strong and confident manner:

> This sudden occurrence in Madhavi's life dried the tears in her eyes. She moved her foot after completely understanding the other. She now learnt to live for herself. She stood erect. Even to this day, she stood with awareness like a lonely star. (Reddy, "Chaitanyam" 81-82)

The western impact has driven away her timidity and turned her into a strong self-dependent woman. The status of the Indian woman continues to be a major debate in contemporary Indian society. In spite of all the advancement in the position of modern women in India, at the attitudinal and behavioural levels, the double standard of morality continues. The modern woman is gradually breaking the shell of narrow existence and rigid traditionalism like Madhavi in "Chaitanyam."

Due to this change in trend, we find such stories written back in India as well. "Bhadratha" (Security) in Volga's *Rajakeeya Kathalu* portrays the protagonist as a sturdy woman who moves away from a bonded troubled life to live a life of her own interest. This story proves that a woman can lead her life without a man by her side. The bonding of a daughter, sister, wife and mother are the burdens laid on a woman by society alone, and these can be traversed. Self-dependent characters are portrayed in today's literature in India by writers who are taking a stance to come out from their cocoons and express the fury existing in their hearts.

So far the woman has looked at the overbearing attitude and highhanded treatment as man's privilege and accepted them with no murmur. But the present-day woman has realized the unjust nature of such attitudes and has started thinking on different lines. For instance, Indu, in Shashi Deshpande's *Roots and Shadows*, takes a bold decision to create her own life. Earlier, the woman lived under the protection of her husband, but the new education has awakened her real self. As a result of this, she starts thinking of an independent and self-dependent life. Indu says, "Sometimes I wonder if I will leave him one day and live by myself. The only way in which I can be myself, my whole self again" (Deshpande, *Roots and Shadows* 97).

"Maa Vidakulu Maavidakulu" (Our Divorce, Mango Leaves) from *Telugu Varadhi* is a beautiful short story written by Bhagavati.[1] Ramarao and Sita, staying in the United States, lack an emotional bonding though happy with their professions. Sita is pictured as a busy woman managing both her office and household work.

Even though women work outside home, they still continue to be regarded as primary caretakers. The home, for Indian immigrants, is the primary sphere in which their cultural identity unfolds. The modern women look at their duty of taking care of and raising their children as important as any professional career. Just as their husbands are seen as "best suited" to compete in the external world of the American workplace, the modern women are regarded as possessing important positions both at office and home: "The company in which Sita worked gained more profits, resulting in the increase of her pay and she overtook Ramarao who joined earlier than her" (Bhagavati, "Maa Vidakulu Maavidakulu" 24).

But at times excessive independence and individualism moulds a person to take wrong decisions. Sita figures out to be disappointed with Ramarao in all the issues including the minute aspects. The subject of family becomes a source of concern for most Indians. In India, if there were any differences between husband and wife, the extended family would have taken a step to solve them. The absence of kith and kin sometimes creates an insecurity misleading them, and particularly the newly-wed, to take hasty decisions.

Sita takes a rapid decision to divorce Ramarao basing on small factors which can be sorted out very easily. Ramarao tries to console Sita and persuade her to take the right decision. He reminds her about traditional customs and the position of being an Indian wife in an American society:

> If we get good contacts here, we can go back to India and develop the required software and send it here. But divorce is not the solution to our problems. If we were in India would the business of divorce arise in your mind? Bhagavati, "Maa Vidakulu Maavidakulu" 26)

This story proves that occasionally, limitless liberty can also be dangerous. But some of the interviews conducted by me had also supported the advantages of being away from the relatives back at home. Indians agreed that they were happy for not having much family pressure in America. They said that it is easier for Indians in America to get out of a relationship or marriage because families are not involved.

The above story is quite different from the other stories looked at earlier. In the previous stories, the proagonists had struggled to maintain their relationships in an alien land where life had become mechanical without the love and affection of their spouses. We have also seen how men and women view marriage differently, with women involving more and doing extra tasks than men. But in "Maa Vidakulu Maavidakulu", we find the opposite, where Sita, an educated and well-settled Indian wife, misuses the fast-paced culture of which she has become a part.

"The Disappearance" in Chitra Banerjee Divakaruni's *Arranged Marriage* is the story of a woman who disappears, leaving her husband and her child behind. This is a completely different story from all the above stories. In most of the stories, the wives are submissive and the husbands in a dominating position. But "The Disappearance" is in contrast to the notion of a husband being an authoritative person:

> He was a good husband. No one could deny it. He let her have her way, indulged her, even. . . . When the kitchen was remodeled, for example, and she wanted pink and gray tiles even though he preferred white . . . "what for, I'm here to take care of you." (Divakaruni, "The Disappearance" 171-172)

Here, the husband fulfills all the needs of his wife to make her happy. The above stories show that it is very uncommon in a marital relationship for the husband to give importance to the wishes of his wife. The difference can also be associated to the background of the individual and the society around him which plays a major influence in formulating his ideas.

In some cases, it would be a mistake to consider that only the wife is submissive and that the purpose behind marriage is merely to enable the husband to bully his wife. The husband is equally submissive towards those who are above him in the hierarchy. When his wife disappears, the husband is shattered and broken. He files a complaint about her disappearance at the police station and also makes every effort to search her:

> WOMAN MISSING read the ad. REWARD $100,000. (How on earth would he come up with that kind of money, asked his friends. The husband confessed that it would be difficult, but he'd manage somehow. His wife was more important to him after all, than all the money in this world.) (Divakaruni, "The Disappearance" 173)

But towards the end, he is shocked to find that his wife had not disappeared suddenly but went away on her own, desolating him for her priorities lie more in her own life than in her family:

> The next day he took the afternoon off from his work, but he didn't go to the doctor. He went to the bank . . . he opened his safety box to find that all the jewelry was gone. She hadn't taken any of the other valuables. (Divakaruni, "The Disappearance" 177)

The author personifies the character from a timid woman to a transformed one taking a drastic step. According to the Indian customs, a wife is to live with her husband until her death following him in all his difficulties and happiness. This applies to the husband also. This concept has undergone a change in this fast-paced country. In this story, there is no proper understanding between the couple. The wife is totally influenced by the colourful world she is in and her confusion arising from this destroys her marital life. We find in this story that excess freedom sometimes results in disaster. In the case of both the protagonists of "Disappearance" and "Maa Vidakulu Maavidakulu", we find them taking swift decisions, thus ruining their marital relationships.

Bharati Mukherjee, an Indian-born American writer, is a familiar voice in the Indian literary diaspora. In her fiction, Mukherjee depicts the problems faced by Indians who attempt to assimilate into the North American lifestyles. *The Middleman and Other Stories* is a collection of short stories that portrays a complete change in the majority of immigrant protagonists. They are seen as immigrants who have fully adapted themselves to American culture. The immigrants of these stories are from India, Italy, Hungary, Vietnam, Afghanistan, etc. We feel that there is a change in the diasporic writing here because the author talks about the whole of immigrant experience and not only of Indians. She talks about the immigrants from different parts of the world facing one major problem, Americanization.

"A Wife's Story" is about a married Indian woman doing her Ph.D. in special education in the United States of America. Panna is a researcher from India. She was never happy with her Indian husband and her strong dominating mother-in-law. She migrates abroad as an excuse from her in-laws. She is scared to think of Indian husbands who burn their wives for dowry: "I've made it; I'm making something of my life. I've left home, my husband to get a Ph. D." (Mukherjee, "A Wife's Story" 29).

She feels happy to be far away in America, far way from all the bonds that have imprisoned her. Bharati Mukherjee's analysis of different American attitudes portrays her notion of Americanization: "It's the tyranny of the American dream that scares me. First you don't exist. Then you're invisible. Then you're funny. Then you're disgusting" (*Ibid*., 26).

She meets Imre, a Hungarian. She feels comfortable with his friendship. He is taken by surprise when Panna hugs him on the road. She thinks such relationships give her confidence. In her own country, Panna would not dare hug her own husband on the road or make friends with other men. But here we find the protagonist happy with her transformation: "That part of my life is over, the way *trucks* have replaced *lorries* in my vocabulary, the way Charity Chin and her lurid love life have replaced inherited notions of marital duty" (*Ibid*., 32).

Panna's husband however is ignorant of the change in his wife. The expression "you're too innocent" is used ironically by the author. But the way Indians are viewed by the American mass media irritates Panna. She silently protests. "Indians don't eat monkey brains" (*Ibid*., 29). This statement of hers brings out the hidden love and respect for her own land. She is still seen as an expatriate, struggling between two worlds or we can also say two values. We see her playing a dual role when her husband visits New York:

> I change out of the cotton pants and shirt I have been wearing all day and put on a sari to meet my husband at JFK. I don't forget the

> marriage necklace or *mangalasutra*, gold drop earrings, heavy gold bangles. I don't wear them every day. In this borough of vice and greed, who knows when, or whom, desire will overwhelm. (*Ibid.*, 33)

This transformation in Panna brings out the nostalgia she has for her land, India. Panna is transformed but she cannot forget her Indian past. The story shows that the marital life of Panna in the past was sick as well as disgusting. Her husband never went out with her in India for shopping because he never recognized her as a person. Only after he comes to the United States he recognizes her as a distinct person with her own identity.

In India, her life was ruled by her mother-in-law and her husband. She did not even call her husband by his first name. His sick and suspicious mentality is known to us through his ironic comments. Such is the strained relationship in this story. In fact Panna is happy to see her husband leaving for India. And again, on the eve of his departure, her role changes into an obedient, loving wife: "Tonight I should make up to him for many years away, the gutted trucks, the degree I'll never use in India. I want to pretend with him that nothing has changed" (*Ibid.*, 40).

Thus the story ends on a note of freedom for an Indian Hindu wife in America, forced because the husband decides to return to India. The story conveys that what is central to married life is the importance of compromise. The author wants to show how traditional Hindu marriage has greater significance than a simple union of man and woman in matrimony. The traditional Hindu concept of marriage is of a sacrament which enables one to fulfill religious as well as social obligations towards the husband. Thus, the protagonist is seen fulfilling her husband's desire on that night, keeping aside her ideals. The author pictures a change in the marital relationship after immigration.

The other story "Tenant" is narrated in the third person. The protagonist Maya Sanyal is an immigrant who leads her life in the present and does not think of the past, that is, does not lead an expatriate's life. Maya Sanyal who has a Ph.D. in comparative literature teaches in Northern Iowa University. She always has a feeling that, "[a] person has to leave home. Try out his wings" (Mukherjee, "Tenant 98), and this statement proves the independent nature of Maya. Maya marries an American and later gets divorced: "'All Indian men are wife beaters,' Maya says. She means it and doesn't mean it. 'That's why I married an American'" (Mukherjee, "Tenant" 99). This brings out the emotion of insecurity in Maya towards Indian men.

She meets Dr. Chatterjee and one Sunday visits his house and family. Her conversation with Dr. Chatterjee portrays him as an expatriate who wants to live and work in America but give back nothing to it except taxes. She hates him because he wants to avoid the confused world of the immigrants and their sense of loss. Dr. Chatterjee's ironical behaviour is evident when he confesses to Maya: "Divorced women can date, they can go to bars and discos. They can see men, many men. But inside marriage there is so much loneliness" (*Ibid.*, 108). The sarcastic behaviour of Dr. Chatterjee becomes so unbearable to Maya that she leaves him. At this juncture, she considers the need of a man, a longing for a suitable relationship. She browses through the matrimonial column and responds to Ashok Mehta, an Indian American. Even though she does not disclose her past relationships, Mehta finds out that she is not free from "problems."

She has to vacate her apartment as her landlord was getting married. She is a "tenant" and not the owner. In fact, she is a tenant in America; her ownership is her motherland, India. But her attempt to become the owner of America proves to be a failure. This gives a picture that though Indians settle in America and inherit its traditions, they still cling on to their roots.

Maya Sanyal wants to stay independent in America and become a free woman. She wants to experience the freedom in her life with free association of men. She not only gives up the Indian way of life but also changes her food habits. This act of hers proves that immigrants need to sacrifice their own culture before they can change into new persons and become one with a new culture. The protagonists of Bharati Mukherjee's stories have to undergo severe problems and suffering to realize the needs and experiences of a new world.

Towards the end Maya Sanyal gets ready to make love to a man without arms. Her entire transformation from the time she entered America breaking away from her parents' way of life to her association with Ashok Mehta, is a long journey of hurdles and of her search for love. In spite of the love she gets, Maya feels the emptiness within her, a feeling of alienation. The author ends the story by picturing the insecure living condition of liberated Indian women in America.

Some writers in India also depict this in their works. The reader notices the emptiness of the protagonist in Shobha De's *Socialite Evenings*, as a liberated Indian woman who is unsatisfied with the fast-paced life and craves for warmth and affection. It is obvious that circumstances and background also play a vital role for the writers to express these views.

Darkness by Bharati Mukherjee is in a sense different from other works of the author. Love, desire and romance as experienced by the immigrant men and women from the Indian sub continent in the new world appear as recurring themes in her collection of short stories, *Darkness*. Unlike the expatriate who experiences nostalgia for the past, the immigrant lives in the present and adjusts herself with the environment around her.

"World according to Hsu" in this collection is a story that stands on marital relationship. This story clearly describes how such relationships are to be based on equality in partnership and mutual understanding. The protagonist is Ratna of Indian origin and her husband Graeme Clayton is a Canadian professor of Psychology at McGill University, Montreal. They are on an island off the coast of Africa. He persuades Ratna to move from what she describes as the "French-dominant-Montreal" to the

"English-dominant-Toronto." Ratna prefers Montreal because in Toronto she would not be an Indian. She would lose her identity. The story reports three incidents of violence against Indians in Toronto supporting her fear. Graeme without giving any heed to Ratna's fear informs her that he has accepted the job in Toronto. He goes alone to Toronto, leaving Ratna behind.

Even though many changes take place in the psyche of Indians after their immigration, some remain the same as they were in their homeland. While some changes are explicitly evident, people do not change in their basic attitudes towards family and marriage. The husband generally remains the sole authority and decision-maker in many cases. The immigrant's dedication to the institution of marriage remains strong and it is viewed as a life-long commitment. Since the husbands and wives come to the United States as adults, their attitudes do not change.

Thus Ratna remains the same even after immigration. Mutual understanding, which is required for a happy married life, is lost in the fast-paced and fluctuating western culture. There is an incident towards the end in which the tourists, confined to the seedy hotel dining room by curfews, dine, listen to each other's conversations and even participate in them:

> Ratna had ordered. "The National Dish." For the first time she saw that the label on the bottle read: Cote de Cassandre. A superior red. . .]. She poured herself another glass, feeling for the moment at home in that collection of Indians and Europeans . . . she would never feel so at home again. (Mukherjee, "World according to Hsu" 53-56)

Many women at the time of marriage hope to go back to their own country after a few years but that has remained a distant dream in many cases. There, they learn to adjust themselves to the alien environment around them. For the women, coming to America is not as adventurous an experience. Most of the women leave India only because their husbands are studying or working in the United States. Few have any control over the issue. They find that as they stay longer, a sense of deep loneliness sets in.

We find two divergent characters in Bharati Mukherjee's short stories "Tenant" and "World according to Hsu." In "Tenant" we see Maya, an immigrant, trying to assimilate herself into the western atmosphere but Ratna in "World according to Hsu," an expatriate, laments over the ex-status of her past. She fails to be an immigrant and clings on to her past traditions and culture. Thus, we find Mukherjee's characterization of the Indian state of mind depicted through the female characters. The characters of Indian men are brought to life through the satiric narratives of immigrant women.

"Clothes" by Chitra Banerjee Divakaruni in *Arranged Marriage* portrays the life of Sumita who is married to Somesh living in California. The author reflects the two images of Sumita in the story. On one hand, she is depicted happy to marry an Indian settled abroad but on the other, she is observed as a confused woman. After her marriage, she tries hard to satisfy her husband in every possible way. As stated earlier, most of the Indian wives' concern is to see that she performs all the services needed by her husband, whose satisfaction is her "pleasure" in life:

> Now his fingers were stroking my cheeks, my throat, moving downward. I closed my eyes and tried not to jerk away because after all it is my wifely duty. (Divakaruni, "Clothes" 21)

Somesh works out in a store along with a partner. The store is open twenty four hours a day. Here the author points out the busy lives of the people in America in contrast to the one back home:

> It stayed open twenty-four hours, yes, all night, every night, not like the Indian stores which closed at dinner time and sometimes in the hottest part of the afternoon. (*Ibid.*, 20-21)

This heavy load of work did not allow the newly married couple to spend time together. They longed to be together, which turned out to be impossible in the fast commercial world they are in: "'Only thing is', Somesh would say about the night shifts, 'I really miss you. I sit there, think of you asleep in bed'" (*Ibid.*, 30).

The protagonist in this story adjusts to the circumstances of her married life. At times, she feels thrown away into an alien world but makes an effort to withstand the impact of western culture and tradition: "I stand inside this glass world, watching helplessly as America rushes by, wanting to scream. Then I'm ashamed. Mita, I tell myself, you're growing westernized. Back home you'd never have felt this way" (*Ibid.*, 26). Towards the end tragedy strikes their wedded life when Somesh gets killed. The "moonlighting" by Somesh becomes the cause of his death and he gets killed by burglars during his night at the store.

Unlike the traditional widow confined to four walls, Sumita does not lose her courage. She gets ready to face future with a strong mind. We notice the transformation of immigrants who face these kinds of problems in America, emerging from grave situations, both due to the influence of the American culture as well as due to an instinct for survival. Contemporary writers in India are also making an attempt to take a stand to represent women who come out of their shells and express their inner thoughts.

During the 1970s and 1980s, the stories have portrayed women as being reliant. But the contemporary writers, especially women writers, prove in their works that women are not timid but outspoken. The change in generation brought a change in their expression. Previously it was thought that only women outside India could express freely because they have no limitations. But today writers in India too are expressing their critical views vividly and explicitly.

Some of the immigrant Indian wives suffer from different kinds of problems. As Indians, they are unable to get rid of their Indian consciousness that they should be honest and true to their marital life. In some of the stories, the Indian married woman is seen as being completely influenced by the Western way of life, resulting in her taking a wrong step. These stories prove that excess liberty can also create problems. There must be a limit to every facet in life to live happily.

"The Ultra Sound" is a story which is different in terms of dealing with the husband and wife relationship. Earlier we have discussed writers dealing with dissimilar issues in a man-woman relationship. But nearly in every story we have arrived at a common point of the husband dominating the wife, both in India and in the fast-paced land, America and the lack of proper understanding between them. But in this story we have an exceptional married couple who support each other in all their joys and sorrows.

This is a story of two friends, Anju and Runu, who are married at the same time. Anju leaves for the United States with Sunil after marriage whereas Runu stays behind in India with a conventional Indian family strongly bound by the Indian customs. Runu is found to be a conservative married Indian woman, serving her husband and the extended family. But Anju is found enjoying her companionship with Sunil away from all the family bondage with no external pressure from her in-laws: "I feel additionally fortunate because in Sunil I've found a friend, someone to discuss the perplexities of America with, someone who understands." (Divakaruni, "Ultra Sound" 213)

She loves sharing her happiness with Runu, whereas Runu is never found revealing her relationship with her husband Ramesh to Anju:

> Runu doesn't say much about her husband. Sometimes I'll ask and a shy note will come into his voice, and she'll change the subject. . . . It is hard for us Indian women to talk openly of love. (*Ibid.*, 214)

At this juncture, Anju seems to be proud of being away from the conservative land, to be in the land of freedom and happiness. On the other hand, Runu stays under the control of her husband

and in-laws. Unfortunately, Runu's in-laws and her husband compel her to get her baby aborted after knowing that the baby is a girl.

Even her own mother does not support Runu in her desire to have the baby. She tries to convince her daughter to obey her in-laws: "She says it's not right that I should leave my husband's home. My place is with them, for better or worse" (*Ibid.*, 225). We notice the life of a subservient Indian wife controlled by the whole world, with no sense of justice. Sometimes the decision-making families in the traditional Indian context become a nagging nuisance to the wife and husband. One has to really get along with the family.

At this instance Anju gets upset and Sunil defends female infanticide saying, "It's a man's world in India" (Divakaruni, "Ultra Sound" 218), and he praises her fortune of being in America, far away from these pressures. He says that the people coming to America have to work only for each other and not for the extended family. Anju imagines what her own status would have been if she were in India and many questions disturb her:

> Would he have cared for me as much if we had been in India and the baby had turned out to be a girl? . . . Would he be asking his parents to look for another wife for him. (*Ibid.*, 228)

But towards the end, she shuts off the arguments and convinces herself that she is happy away from family burdens. Most of the immigrant wives feel that they enjoy more privacy in the United States as compared to India, since they have their husbands all to themselves, with no one intruding upon their lives.

The entire story is the difference between the same people who were born and brought up in one culture but staying in two different lands. The story proves that their ideas and ways of thinking depend on where they are located. While one enjoys the fruit of immigration staying in an alien land far away from foolish superstitions, the other is bound by them.

"Affair" is the story of two different women, one accustomed to the western impact and the other still clinging on to past traditions. Meena gets habituated to the fast culture around her. She works and dresses in the western way whereas Abha remains the same. Abha engages herself by writing Indian recipes for magazines.

Here the author shows the reasons for the conversion of a traditional Indian woman into a westernized person, responding to questions that have cropped up earlier. We have argued many times that the fast-paced land affects the traditionalism of the Indians. But in this story, the author brings out the suffering and loneliness of a married Indian woman searching for some companionship that would keep her occupied. Meena, when she is married and migrates to the United States, experiences the loss and absence of her husband, though he is in America:

> I used to be dreadfully jealous when we were first married. Srikant would stay on at work till all kinds of hours, even though I kept telling him I hated being alone in the house. It was deathly quiet, not like India. (Divakaruni, "Affair" 239)

Back in India, her kith and kin would have kept her occupied but the sudden emptiness of the new world shatters her life. This is not only what Meena experiences but it is what most married Indian women in America undergo: "*It's what all of us Indian wives went through*" (*Ibid.*, 239). When Meena endures this, Abha too feels the same. Abha who cannot get rid of her timidity could not satisfy Ashok in his expectations of being a modern Indian wife:

> Early in our marriage, once or twice, he'd suggested doing things differently, trying something new. . . . But I'd reacted with such undisguised horror that he hadn't brought it up again. (*Ibid.*, 244)

We find both the primary characters in the story unhappy with their marital relationships. Meena searches out for her own happiness with an extra-marital affair, bringing an end to her uncomfortable life with Srikant. In the circumstances, there is the disadvantage of not having near and dear ones in an alien land to direct the person onto the right path. According to conventional traditional norms, the wife is supposed to serve her husband and adjust her relationship with him; giving less importance to her own interests. Her priority should be for the family. Here we observe that she likes to have her choice of life rather than struggle under the wings of her husband. This change is not an influence of the western impact alone but also due to the changed dimensions of the transformed traditions that have made the writers take up such concepts to develop their arguments.

Meena is not bound by traditional rules and wishes to live a life of her own. Though initially Abha disagrees with Meena's choice, she later gives it a thought and towards the end we find Abha changed:

> *The old rules aren't always right. Not here not even in India. . . .* And Srikant—no, I won't think about him now. There'll be time enough for that later on, when I've begun to pull the unravelled edges of my existence into a new design, one I cannot guess at yet. (*Ibid.*, 270-72)

Abha moulds her life according to her wish. In this story we find the timid, self-effacing woman transforming into a bold one, seeking her own life, while breaking the old traditional rules.

Arranged Marriage is Chitra Banerjee Divakaruni's first collection of short stories, focusing on women from India caught between two worlds. The characters are both liberated and trapped by cultural changes, struggling to carve out an identity of their own. Chitra Banerjee Divakaruni deals with a variety of issues in the book, including racism, interracial relationships, economic disparity, abortion and divorce. She says that the stories are inspired by her imagination and the experience of others. Her writing often centers on the lives of immigrant women.

The immigrant's commitment to the institution of marriage remains strong and it is viewed as a lifelong commitment. Since the husbands and wives have come to the United States as adults, it is only to be expected that their attitudes would not change after migration. Thus, it is seen that Indians even in an alien world are attuned to Indian culture despite their struggle between the strict old traditions and the challenge provided by their new life.

Most of the stories we have discussed above, present the difficulties faced by the Indian wives in an alien culture without the company of friends or relatives, while struggling to cope with the new surroundings they cannot call their home. Most Indian immigrants remain convinced that love is of great importance in sustaining a marital relationship. Even the fantasy world of America does not change the marital life of the immigrants.

The stories we have dealt with so far make it clear that most Indian men in the diaspora, according to these writers, generally remain the same. There is little change in their attitudes or manners. Husbands try to rule over their wives in most cases. Very few women enjoy freedom after marriage in a foreign country. Even the fast-paced culture around them does not change men in their approach towards their wives. The practice of the husband and wife spending time together remains a vision even today, says Kavitha Murthy in her dissertation, "Inter Generational Comparison of Love and Marriage among Asian Indians: A Qualitative Inquiry." Some women use the advantages America provides, while some misuse them, spoiling their inter-personal relationships.

Recent literature in India on desirable qualities preferred in a potential mate indicates that gradual changes are occurring in Indian society regarding the conception of marriage. As Indian society is gradually being subjected to the influence of urbanization and westernization, marriage is viewed from a more personalized and individualized perspective. As such, we can see even in the works of writers writing in India, the impact of westernization, especially in the way they dealt with sensitive issues. But the only difference lies in their mode of expression.

The above analysis makes it obvious that the woman strives for an ideal relationship. The writers writing both in Telugu and English state that it should not be forgotten that man-woman relationship cannot be restored to the axis of equality through liberty alone but through mutual understanding, love, respect, and dilution of egos. Writers writing abroad, especially Telugu writers, are least bothered about their mode of expression. Telugu writers at times write just to pass time and as well to preserve their language and culture. Neither do they fear any one. But writers writing in India are concerned with every minute aspect of their expression. Their works are often criticized severely and thus they fear articulating their thoughts as easily as diasporic writers.

Telugu writers writing in America do not write with the aim of making money, whereas writers in India write to earn from their works. Thus, they cannot express their emotions as openly as diasporic writers do. Therefore, we find differences between works of both kinds of writers. This difference exists in writings in the regional language and writings in English also. Some writers writing in English are seen as more rebellious in their mode of expression compared to the writers in Telugu. Short stories in English seem to link diasporic literature with the mainstream. The characters are reconciled to their positions and are stable. They are ready to accept western influence and convert themselves into independent persons.

To sum up, the position of the woman in general and Indian woman in particular has been paradoxical. That is, she has been the key person, the main figure in the family, and yet she has lived the life of subjugation, suffering and suppression. However, now she has started becoming conscious of her rights, responsibilities and destination. Presently, the period she is passing through is a transitional one.

Though works in Telugu too follow the same chosen path, they differ in their expression. The characters are sublime in their relationships. They are still undergoing the pressure of coming out into the vast space where they can stand on their own. Most of the Telugu stories we have dealt with in this chapter reflect the emotional fulfillment and companionship of the families. Even though they express their fearless comments on the way western culture and tradition mould their lives, somewhere lurks a panic in the stories. They do write freely but the concept of regional reprimand haunts them, and this is reflected in their short stories.

"Regional reprimand" pertains to the regional writers especially when compared to writers writing in English like Bharati Mukherjee. Though writers in Telugu are free to express their fearless comments on the influence of western culture and tradition, the thought of the regional audience obstructs them from using strong emotions or feelings. They cannot articulate like Bharati Mukherjee while expressing the concept of love or the sexual element. As her readership includes an international audience which is exposed to such themes, her works are concerned with these notions; these are, however, rare in Indian writers, especially regional writers.

Regional writing is limited only to their own regional speaking audience whereas English writing reaches all, including the international audience. Thus some of the diasporic works in English try to reach out like Bharati Mukherjee's short stories and novels. The Telugu woman writer is not so liberated as to express the concept of love and marriage as openly as Bharati Mukherjee does in English.

One important aspect that differentiates Telugu writing from English writing in America is the age of the writers. Most Telugu writers are in their middle age, if not old. To the best of my knowledge, there are no real young writers writing in Telugu from the United States of America. This age factor may be reflected in the stories too.

Not surprisingly, Indian gender norms also shape the migration pattern of those Indians who enter the United States as immigrants. While some stories reflect Indian women having more independence in the United States, some others depict marital violence. While gender relations between immigrant Indian men and women tend to change in the United States, mostly to the benefit of women, the isolation from family, friends, and relatives have a significant effect on man-woman relationship.

Thus immigration is a mixed blessing for Indians in the United States. On the one hand they have to handle the new changes and inculcate past traditions in the younger generation. Thus the conflict of being alienated from their peers, while at the same time, being forced to live "double and fractured lives," both at home and American society, is what we read in the next chapter.

NOTE

1. Her biographical details are not known from any source.

Chapter 3

Indian at Home and American Outside: Inter-Generational Conflicts

The word diaspora in some sense is intentional in the narratives of the second generation. The term itself derives from a long-standing history specifying to Jewish ideas of exile and redemption. Even the term second generation implies to people twice removed from their homeland and their origin. There is a strong conviction among parents that the only way they can protect their children from their predicament is to make sure that they have a good professional career.

In studying how Indian values are transmitted from one generation to the next, an essential variable for examination becomes parent-child relationship. When we talk about close family values, certain themes emerge—the role of the parents in caring for the children including providing education for them and arranging their marriage, teaching respect to children and imparting a collective identity, the role of the children in caring for their elderly parents, the importance of maintaining contact with the family in India. Though the parents migrate for the development of their children, it is surprising to note the conflicts that arise between first- and second-generation immigrants. In dealing with this theme, let us focus deeply into the short stories written by diasporic Indian women in America.

Identity tends to be related to the length of stay in the United States and to the sense of being established there. As these Indian immigrants become settled in the United States, they tend to resort to their regional identities. Identity is also contextual, depending upon the environment they find themselves in and the degree of familiarity others have of Asian Indian culture. Most parents with advanced education, both men and women, view the western value of freedom of choice and the American value of questioning traditions as positive and something they want to implant in the second generation.

Examining gender differences is also important in the parent-child relationship. Parents are always well-wishers of their children. It is their natural instinct that their children should get respectable and well-paid positions in their career. In general, most of the second-generation immigrants feel confident of their abilities and have an optimistic outlook towards life. But, sometimes we find the second generation feeling guilty of not being able to follow their culture. They are also troubled because they find themselves constrained and controlled in different ways. The pressure they experience in this regard varies. Most of these young people feel that experiences of racism are painful and humiliating. Some of them recall the trauma they went through particularly as children in grade school where going to school was an ordeal because of being bullied.

Parents in general try to transmit their culture through making their children participate in cultural activities and have frequent interactions with other families within their group that celebrate festivals and other cultural meets. The expectation is that the second generation will naturally imbibe cultural tenets as they attend cultural meets and participate in family activities. There is a strong conviction among parents that the only way they can protect their children is to make sure that they have good professions. The understanding is that professional qualifications will make them less vulnerable to prejudice and discrimination. A more secure job provides a better cushion against the racism of life in a society that is usually unfriendly towards their children and often hostile.

This chapter explores the concepts of culture, identity, and processes of identity formation and retention among first- and second-generation immigrants from a literary perspective. Research on Asian Indian ethnic groups is by and large concentrated on the first-generation immigrants. Their studies have elaborated the concerns and preoccupations of this generation and have identified their pattern of adaptation to a larger society. But the cultural difficulties of the second generation are hardly talked about. These are representative stories by diasporic Indian women who are first-generation writers. Thus the problems are indicated from the point of view of the parents alone. Most of the stories try to justify their concept of parent-child relationships.

"Abhaasulu-Abhaathulu"[1] (American Indian Children-American Indian Parents) from *America Telugu Kathanika* is a short story written by Pudipedhi Seshu Sarma. The story with a well-connected plot discusses the conflicts of the first and second generations in America. This story has powerful arguments between parents and children. It deals with all the Indian Telugu families who gather for a get-together to celebrate their migrant status in America. The centre of attraction turns out to be a special session for the second generation to express their views liberally, for or against their diasporic status.

Many of the second-generation participants in the story convey their views emphatically about the inconsistencies in their day-to-day living in America:

> But you don't remember that we are brought up in America. You don't recognize the fact that there is no relationship between your needs when you were at our age and of our needs here being raised in western culture. (Sarma, "Abhaasulu-Abhaathulu" 11)

The second generation is particularly irritated by parental insistence that the children live their lives exactly as they did in India when they were growing up. They consider it unrealistic to expect that children who are raised in America have the same outlook towards life as their parents who were raised in an entirely different environment. The parents fail to acknowledge the differences between the two generations. The reasoning of children behind such a stance is that the first generation chose to immigrate to America and they are ready to play by their own rules:

> You came to America to enjoy all the comforts in this country. It is injustice if you wish to raise us as you were raised in India twenty five years back. (*Ibid.*, 11)

This is the general notion of all the second-generation immigrants who undergo the turmoil of hanging between two worlds. They want their parents to leave them alone, away from the culture that bonds them and to recognize the generation gap:

> Parents, I want you to know something. You are Indians but we are Americans. You may think we are American born confused Desis. But we are not Desis. We are Americans. (*Ibid.*, 11)

This argument exists in almost all of the second-generation immigrants who state that they belong to the country that they are born into.

As the story proceeds with the opinions of the children, the parents in the story are agitated about their children who have expressed their views against them:

> We came to this country just as we were, worked hard day and night, saved money, studied, achieved a good life and gave birth to you. We struggled so you could be happy and that is our mistake. Do you know how our lives are? Like doldrums. (*Ibid.*, 12)

Most of the sociologists[2] say that the first generation works very hard to go out of their way to ensure that their children study well and achieve the goal of successful careers. They have struggled very hard to raise their children in an alien land with no emotional support from the family. They want their children to realize the difficulties they had experienced and to maintain their traditions. While the first-generation immigrants tend to attach to the Indian culture with hope and energy, the second and subsequent generations show evidence of distancing themselves from it:

> It's true, if you have noticed or not, these parents are in such a state that they don't know what they or their children are doing. They are bringing up their children neither like the American parents nor like Indian parents. (*Ibid.*, 13)

First-generation Indian immigrants are either conservative or open enough to adapt themselves completely towards western modes of life. Looking at the western atmosphere and culture, some parents fear for their children's future, as they compare it to the life back in India. The fear leads them to control the second generation. This becomes a nagging nuisance to the children who are strangers to their original homelands. This cap of westernization on their heads and the culture they are born into confuse them.

Finally Seshu Sarma tries to say that the parents should trust the children and let them organize their own lives. It is important that parents should trust their children and the children should give importance and respect to their parents. The author's humorous title "Abhaasulu-Abhaathulu" states the difference of "American Indian kids" and "American Indian parents." The title signifies the confusion of both the first and the second generations.

"Pelli Chesukunte Chudu" (See if I'll Marry) from *America Telugu Kathanika* is another story by Pudipedhi Seshu Sarma which signifies the fear of parents in nurturing the children. The perception of their children getting married in an American society is a nightmare for many of the Indian parents. Since arranged marriage is the dominant system traditionally followed by their ethnic group, there is a strong tendency to favour this system. This preference is justified on the basis of "parents know best", because of their age and experience.

Many immigrant parents believe that the strength of their own relationship rests upon the success of an arranged marriage system because they see a high rate of divorce among Americans as evidence of the failure of "love" marriages and they discourage their children from dating classmates and their friends. For many children, such a practice seems overly restrictive. The issue of dating thus has been cast as the biggest source of tension between parents and children:

> "These days we are not the ones to get them married. Most importantly, if we think of a wedding, we will be made to undergo a lot of trauma. Getting them married is a task beyond our imagination," Sarada said with a sigh. (Sarma, "Pelli Chesukunte Chudu" 35)

Sarada, the protagonist in the story is noticed as a worried mother, trying to find an alliance for her twenty-one-year-old daughter. She assumes that the American atmosphere might transform her daughter with its western impact and she wants to avoid that stage. Respect for age and experience is expected from the youngsters. In addition, the system of arranged marriages is considered preferable particularly in the case of daughters. Since virginity before marriage is considered important and since family honour is tied to the daughter's moral conduct, parents consider it their duty to protect their daughters.

Sarada is a mother who tries to be overprotective towards her daughter, thus compelling her to marry a person from their own community. But the father is seen as a different person who remains calm for he recognizes the possibilities of the American marriage system. Gopalrao understands his daughter well and supports her decision of further studies and her determination of settling down in life before marriage. He consoles his wife, asking her to be happy, for their daughter has not yet been Americanized:

> It's not my stupidity. It's your craziness. In a country and a time when name, sex, marriages are on a rampage in the developed world, if my beloved daughter comes to me and says, 'Dad, I am marrying this guy', I will consider that to be a great blessing. (*Ibid.*, 36)

Here we see the father as a socially aware person. He is quite different from his wife in his thinking. But the mother who lives in a cocoon, that is, who considers home as her world, finds it difficult to face the realities of life.

Apart from this, the parents encourage friendships of their children among their own communities to increase the likelihood of marrying within the culture so as to preserve the regional identity. Most of the parents at least hope that their children would choose a spouse from their own region. Majority of women from the group I interviewed stated that if their children do not marry a person from their community or region, it makes no difference if they marry an Indian or an American. "They are both foreigners," they stated, citing language and regional identity as the major variables. Emphasizing the importance of one's own value system, the mother in the story says:

> We don't have any objection if they themselves choose their own spouse. But we would be happy if our customs and traditions match. (*Ibid.*, 37)

Many parents on one hand support the dating system and on the other, they aspire to preserve their culture. Many parents are ready to allow their children considerable freedom when this is necessary for the happiness of the second generation. But they may still demand that the children should behave in a very conservative manner at home. One important reason for parents forcing their children in this regard is to continue their family line.

Most of the second-generation immigrants tend to compartmentalize their lives living as Indians at home and as Americans outside, which is unhealthy for both the children and their parents:

> Our kids are Americans. I am scared that we may force them without giving them the choice. Our kids will say that they would meet and talk to them to wipe away our tears. But they have a low opinion of our decisions and choices. (*Ibid.*, 35)

Children leading an Indian life at home and an American one outside does not account for a generational difference. It illustrates how the American-born children only mimic their immigrant parents' behaviour, without consciously carving out a different identity.

This is just not one story that generalizes the concept of differences between the first and the second generations, but there are instances where we find the second generation mimicking their parents like Gita in Sarma's "Sangarshana" and many more. My whole idea is to discuss and portray different views on the conflicts by exploring different stories rather than concentrating on one end and this therefore makes me pick a few cases for illustration. On the whole the stories represent the parents' dual task of imparting mainstream American culture and of stressing the need to maintain their own customs and traditions. The notion that the second generation is likely to suffer from culture conflicts is a gross over-simplification of a wide range of complex personal experiences.

It assumes a straightforward clash, a tug-of-war between east and west, traditional and modern, rural and urban, repression and freedom, resulting in an unbridgeable gulf between generations. In the story discussed above, the author seems to write out of her own experience of being an Indian mother in a western land. The story portrays the difficulties of diasporic Indian parents' struggle in getting their children married to a person of their own choice. On the other hand, it also portrays problems of the second generation, struggling to satisfy their parents as well as themselves.

"Sangarshana" (Conflict) from *America Telugu Kathanika* by Pudipedhi Seshu Sarma is another beautiful story which reflects the confusion of the second generation's struggle between two cultures. It is a story of Gita born in America and familiar with Indian customs. Though accustomed to Indian traditions and culture, Gita finds it difficult to practise them as a second-generation immigrant. Each of her acts in regard to tradition is based on her parents' compulsion. She visits temples as an obligation but cannot convince herself to admit it:

> Mom, people like you who have blind faith in God . . . that is why they are spending millions of dollars constructing huge temples and worshipping, but in our case. . . . Our generation is least interested in worshipping. What can I teach my kids? (Sarma, "Sangarshana" 92)

The problems of second-generation Indians in the United States are discussed primarily on the assumption that there are major and increasingly irresolvable conflicts between the children and their parents. The emphasis is placed on the incompatibility of Indian and western cultures and on the discontinuities and contradictions in the behaviour and aspirations of the second generation. It is widely believed that the people of the second generation grow up among their American friends and challenge the authoritarian repressiveness of their own parents. They are seen as a rootless generation caught between two worlds.

Asian Indian youth tend to begin searching and resolving their identity by the time they reach college. At this stage, they become confused about their identity as Indians and Americans. They begin to question more of the customs they grew up with, such as temple worship or the exclusive use of Brahmin priests in temples. However, the underlying structure of a desire for a Telugu identity or family identity remains intact. Gita struggles in this kind of a situation, unable to identify herself.

If this is the case of Gita, there's Jyoti, a second-generation immigrant who is not hurdled by Indian customs. She has liberty given by her parents to choose a life of her interest, for they believe that their daughter would ultimately marry an Indian:

> Recently my brother's friend Nagabhushanam's daughter married an American. . . . "Jo" was brought up with a western outlook. They have never conformed to our culture or our religion. But still they thought that it would have been nice if she married a Hindu or

> at least an Indian. How much ever we change, our outlook remains the same where our children's marriage is concerned (*Ibid.*, 90)

Some parents who understand the need for change and are capable to communicate the reason for their attitudes to their children are able to strike a balance between being a strict disciplinarian and giving in to all their children's demands. As such some families share a deep religious faith, and both parents and children are able to accept these differences peacefully and to maintain mutual respect and affection.

During the interviews, most of the parents spoke about the autonomy of American children. For them the guiding principle of parenting is to allow freedom of choice to the children. They say that in America one cannot expect children to live by the same rules as they would have done in their home. For most parents this liberty is a mixed bag. For, sometimes some of the choices their children make do not concur with the parents' wishes. This view is brought out clearly in the text mentioned earlier:

> The characters of the three men that I met till now are not similar to mine . . . but between me and the person that I marry there should be harmony in all respects. If not, our married life would be short. After the kids are born, we should stand firm on one opinion, especially about their upbringing. (*Ibid.*, 92)

The second generation is concerned about its own psychological well-being. It is an experimental generation expected to chart its own course of adaptation or assimilation, as it lacks role models within its own ethnic group. Many questions confuse the second generation in a "home" that does not belong to them. Whom will they marry? How will they reconcile their bi-cultural values? To what degree will they pass their Indian culture to the third generation? These are questions that trouble most of the second-generation immigrants.

I feel that these questions trouble them because the American-born Indian generation cannot but be a replica of their parents. Developing an Indian identity is based on immigrants' memories of a homeland and the sense of isolation that they feel in the United States. The feeling for India is of a lesser intensity to those who did not grow up there; thus, the second generation questions the concept of a strong "Indian life." So, the difference between immigrants and their children is based less on generation gap than on the role of memory in recreating the relationship between parents and children in India.

"Sangarshana" is a story where the second generation questions the first about the possibility of leading a life of an Indian in a westernized milieu. The parents insist on the second generation to learn the culture of their homeland by participating in activities promoted by Indian organizations. Indian immigrants are from a society where tradition rules the life and acts as a guide to a right living. But the second generation questions the significance and use of such outdated rules and customs. Ravindra K. Jain in his book, *Indian Communities Abroad* says, "parents want to maintain the traditional authority structure in their families and often ignore the fact that the child's socialization is highly influenced by the environment outside the family" (67).

Radhika Nori is another writer who gives equal importance to relationships in a foreign land. Most of her stories deal with marital relationships, parent-child relationships and family values. "Viluvalu" (Values) from *America Telugu Kathanika* is a beautiful story constructed on the views of first and second generations, the attempt of a mother in leading her son on the right path with manifestations of an in-built Indian culture.

There is a general tendency among first-generation immigrants to consider their own cultural values as superior to those of the dominant culture of North American society. They look down upon the uncontrolled individualism of the west and instead privilege family values of their ethnic culture. Moreover, they expect their children to cherish those values. We can see it reflected in the following words:

> I have been living here before you. So I am more knowledgeable about this country's customs and traditions. I am not asking about the customs here. I am reminding you of our customs and traditions . . . do you remember any of the values that inculcated in your childhood? (Nori, "Viluvalu" 15)

Maintaining the past culture while still being bonded with the present bothers the second generation. The second generation is of the opinion that ethnic cultural values should be observed in the privacy of home and out in the society they should adjust to mainstream values and not create a huge issue regarding these differences:

> "Mom! It is said 'Be like a Roman, when you are in Rome!' Do you know how odd it would be if I behave in a different way when I am with everyone." Naveen said with anger. (*Ibid.*, 15)

There are many parallels between the critical and rebellious attitudes of Indian and western adolescents. They argue with their parents about the same things and at the same time under pressure they criticize their parents' rejection of American cultural values. They become less keen to accept the unquestioned beliefs and assumptions of their parents, particularly as their education encourages them to demand explicit rationale for everything.

Here the author infuses her own personality into the character of the protagonist. She as a first-generation immigrant plays the role of a mother through the character. This story does not imitate the other stories where parents and children fight over susceptible issues resulting in a conflict. The mother here plays a vital role in communicating her views to her son in leading him onto a proper track. She has never been a hurdle in her son's freedom and has given everything that her son has aspired for. But she reminds him that every action has a borderline and one should be very cautious not to cross it:

> Just to be like everyone, should we go against our values . . . and follow their customs? Though we are in a different land moving with different people there is no necessity for us to forget our cul-

> ture and traditions. We need to draw a line where we need to. (*Ibid.*, 15-16)

Many parents allow their children to enjoy the westernized life of America but at the same time expect them to maintain their own tradition:

> Though we undergo many pressures we should never forget our identity. Nor should we lose it. I taught you to mingle with different people to learn these things. . . . For you to be exposed to diversified cultures, I saw to it that you had American friends along with Indian ones, and black friends with white ones. (*Ibid.*, 16)

Parents are rather uncompromising regarding core values but are relatively more accommodating where some aspects of Indian tradition are concerned. They are also ready to give more freedom of movement and career choice. But the tendency of maintaining their ethnic culture also exists:

> I only told you not to forget our customs and traditions wherever and with whoever you are. Because, customs and traditions to everyone are like a water flow. It should flow continuously without any hindrances. (*Ibid.*, 15)

Finally, the mother is successful in changing her son and making him understand the mainstream American culture and a need for him to maintain his own customs and traditions. She proves that interacting with two systems provides one a useful way of understanding culture and society as well as the concept of identity that emerges through an interaction between the person and the environment. But in general, the second generation tends to be sensitive to cultural differences.

This is also reflected in Bharati Mukherjee's short story, "Father" in *Darkness*. Mr. Bhowmick in the story is a well-disciplined man. He is a person who feels that certain matters can be first planned and later put into practice to lead a comfortable life. Earlier, we have seen him as a failure in his marital relationship. Now, we see him as a failure in the role of a father:

"The women in his family were smarter than him. They were cheerful, outgoing, more American somehow" (Mukherjee, "Father" 61).

In this family it is surprisingly women who are outspoken, colourful, courageous and more Americanized. I say surprisingly because many times it is men who have to acculturate to America because they get more exposure into the society with an advantage of working outside for not many women in our stories are employed. In most of the stories, a lot of women live within their own world creating a cocoon, clinging to past traditions and culture unlike Mrs. Bhowmick and her daughter. "Father" is a story of a father who has never had a positive notion about his daughter:

> Babli was not the child he would have chosen as his only heir, she was brighter certainly than the sons and daughters . . . but as she sat there in her beige linen business suit, her thick chin dropping into a polka dotted cravat, he regretted again that she was not the child of his dreams. (*Ibid.*, 63)

Babli, his daughter is not the child he had thought of. He feels that she is truly an intelligent daughter who can help her father in financial crisis but not one who can comfort him. He never finds her feminine either physically or mentally:

> But Babli could never comfort him. She wasn't womanly or tender the way that unmarried girls had been in the wistful days of his adolescence. Not the kind that had given him palpitations in Ranchi. (*Ibid.*, 63)

This strengthens our case that first-generation immigrants are uprooted, drawn or pushed to the American shores, but are forever ill-adapted in terms of language, values and cultural practices to the change. Their hopes lie in the second generation who master the language and the ways of the new society. But their children adapt themselves at the cost of rejecting the parents' way of life, or at least by subordinating it.

The father is portrayed as a traditional person, who is always found clinging to the past customs in an alien world and who cannot digest the truth about his daughter. On a fine day when he finds his unmarried daughter pregnant, he feels happy for her and even tries to console himself with the fact of her not being married. He looks forward to his grandson: "He pictured his grandson crawling to him, and the grandson was always fat and brown and buttery-skinned, like the infant Krishna" (*Ibid*., 70)

This is a positive aspect of the story, for when the father observes that his daughter is pregnant, he gets ready to accept it and awaits the gift of a grandchild. He is not worried about the caste and creed of her man but just shows his anxiety to have a grandchild. The positive feeling suddenly turns to a brutal one when he hears that the cause of his daughter's pregnancy is not a man but artificial insemination. This is because his daughter hates men: "'Who needs a man?' She hissed. 'The father of my baby is a bottle and a syringe. Men louse up your lives. I just want a baby'" (*Ibid*., 72).

Shocked, he hits the daughter with a rolling pin on her stomach. The act of the father tells us that he could not accept the reality of his failure in the role of a "father." This story reflects the strained relationship between the father and the daughter. We see him both as a coward husband and a coward father who can neither convince his wife nor "control" his daughter. This incident sets young Indians as a "problematic" category confused with two traditions. We fail to recognize that there can be a comparable degree of conflict between parents and children in families of any cultural background.

It does not take into account either the particular personalities of individuals or their various material and social circumstances. A lot depends on the way parents raise their children. We see the father in the story shunning the responsibilities. He fails to be a father to his daughter as far as her needs were concerned but tries to take control of her views and deeds. This control is not vindicated as he was never a responsible father. At this juncture he cannot expect his daughter to listen to his suggestions and lead what he considers a proper path, while he failed to be a reliable parent. We saw Radhika Nori in "Viluvalu" representing a mother who at the right moment induces responsibility in her son to live a life of significance towards their culture but in this story we find the father averting responsibilities when needed.

It is the mother in "Viluvalu" who is worried about the son and here it is the father who is worried about the daughter. Generally we find that the mother is a responsible person in the welfare of the children and family while the father is a bread-winner. The mother's traditional role is to be an example to her children to follow and to act as a mediator between them and their father. In some families the mother finds it difficult to pass on behavioral norms to her children especially when she is away from her land and is overwhelmed by domestic responsibilities as is the case of Mrs. Bhowmick. She may find herself unable to understand, let alone answer her children's questions or act as a mediator between them and their father.

The modern culture has moulded Babli into a "stubborn" woman who does not feel the need of a man. Babli who has never had any interaction with her parents has no awareness about her native customs. She has been born and brought up in America, its traditions making her independent and strong even when she had no affection or moral support. Generally, an Indian reader tends to view such strong character as a "stubborn" one: "Girls like Babli were caught between rules, that's the point he wished to make. They were too smart, too impulsive for a backward place like Ranchi, but not tough nor smart enough for sex-crazy places like Detroit" (Mukherjee, "Father" 72).

Babli tries to be an independent woman, neither a daughter nor a wife. We do not find emotional bonds or sentiments in this story, as we generally find in the works of Indian writers. Maybe it is because the author of the story is also an immigrant woman who has been undergoing such emotional conflicts that helped her out to be strong and outspoken. The story proves that while struggling between traditions and cultures of the land they have left behind and the alien one they have inherited, many lose the emotional bond.

When the daughter says that she does not need a man but needs a child, it pricks Bhowmick's conscience and he hits her. He, as a man, is shocked at the statement because he is a "failed father", a "father" who could not show his parental love to his daughter. The daughter who lost the warmth and affection finds herself in the clutches of American culture.

"Kaagala Kaaryam Gandharvule Theerchaaru" (The Gandharvas Themselves Completed the Possible Task) from *America Telugu Kathanika* by Radhika Nori is a well-developed story. The whole story is based on the conflicts of first and second generations and deals with the arguments between parents and children. This story has similarities with "Viluvalu" by the same writer. The story starts with a good construction of relationships and at the end we see a transformation of the second generation realizing the importance of one's own customs and traditions.

Nischala and Somayaajulu lead a happy life with their children Rakesh and Rajini till Lara enters their life. Lara, Rakesh's girlfriend, visits their house to meet his family. Somayaajulu, a conventional father, disapproves the decision of his son dating an American, but finally agrees satisfying Rakesh's wish, concealing his.

Children of Indian families born in the United States seem to adapt more easily to western society, despite resistance from parents. This, of course, causes an inevitable gap between parents and children. As such, children of these immigrants appear to be more assimilated into the western culture than their parents. This results in a certain type of ambivalence among parents about how to cope with and continuously modify their traditional value systems. Immigrant parents perceive the real pressure of westernization in some sensitive areas, such as their children's associations with the opposite sex, and the issues of dating and marriage, which conflict with the traditional Indian method of match-making.

Though Somayaajulu endorses Rakesh's wish he is yet disappointed with his son's educational background. Somyaajulu being a doctor by profession desires his son to continue in the same field. Parents tend to be demanding of their children, especially in terms of their educational achievement. Even though parents point out to successful Indian doctors or engineers as role models for their children, these are not necessarily careers that the children want to follow:

> Why do you always raise the issue of my education? Apart from medicine and engineering, aren't there other courses? Are these two the only road to a successful and happy life? (Nori, "Kaagala Kaaryam Gandharvule Theerchaaru" 76)

We see that the second generation, as a result, feels boxed in by their parents' expectations. They feel that they are forced to do everything according to their parents' wishes. They do not understand that their parents' aspirations help them settle in their lives. They, in fact, feel they are burdened with their parents' ambitions.

For immigrants and their children, normal and expected family tensions are compounded by the fact that these families maintain an almost "schizophrenic" existence, attempting to straddle two different and strong cultures:

> I don't have any specific ill-feeling towards the Americans. But our religion, our culture, our traditions, our customs are all different . . . if there are so many diversities, how can a married life be happy and peaceful. (*Ibid.*, 78)

Parents bring with them cultural attitudes and expectations towards marriage from the old country and desire to have a degree of social control over marital practices. Indian immigrants are generally expected to marry within their ethnic group, an attitude reinforced by the behaviour of the dominant group. They also extend a higher degree of control over dating and marital practices through appeals of family solidarity and family name.

They may date but when the question of marriage comes up, they expect them to marry within the ethnic group. Inter-racial, inter-ethnic and inter-religious marriages are allowed only under special circumstances. Parents are rather uncompromising regarding the above-mentioned core values but are relatively more accommodating with regard to dress, food habits as well as language spoken at home:

> Nischala! Like many other kids of today, Rakesh also doesn't know his needs. However, he doesn't even know what he doesn't want. . . . They say, "Who are you to tell us? Our life, our decisions, our wishes." (*Ibid.*, 76)

This is not just with Rakesh and his parents but with most of the first- and second-generation immigrants in the United States. Findings[3] suggest that the second generation is proud of its ethnic culture but does not like the practice of sexual double standards followed by their parents. In general, the youth do view the dominant culture as having a corrupting influence on them. They experience conflict even though there is a difference in the intensity of the conflict, the form it takes, as well as the type of accommodation arrived at.

Soma Sudeshana Reddy's "Mogudu Kavaala" (Want a Husband) in *America Telugu Katha* beautifully describes the objective of a mother in trying to find good alliances for her daughters. Janaki and Raghava stay in the United States with their four daughters. Generally, in India, parents in collaboration with other elderly relations and friends start planning their children's marriage well ahead of time. Parents decide who, where and when they should marry. Thus, in a society like India, where the joint family system is the norm, marriages are largely arranged by parents and their elders:

> When the girls attain the age of marriage, we do not know what to do, can't sit with folded hands, can't forcibly bend their heads (you know what I mean), no mood to get them married . . . oh!! . . . They say it's just like between earth and heaven. (Reddy, "Mogudu Kavaala" 156)

Here we notice the Indian parents of American-born children struggling alone to arrange good matches in a land where they lack the support of their families. Janaki makes every effort to see her elder daughter Seema married to an Indian. Staying in a western land, they neither dare to take strong decisions to formulate their children's lives nor do they strive to bring success to their own. Other than achieving economic independence, the author pictures the parents as a failure in major issues especially when related to their children.

On one side when parents have their own problems in raising their children, the second generation on the other face the problems of being caught between two worlds, the one they live and the other they have left behind:

> "He is our relative's son. You wouldn't know whether you like him or not unless you meet him. . . ." Seema lamented frequently struggling between two different lives. (*Ibid.*, 157)

The second generation hangs amidst two lands capitulated with the traditional norms not belonging to either of them.

Parents tend to fulfill their dreams through their children but generally do not attempt to recognize their interests. The following conversation describes the turmoil of Seema in the story, trapped by the emotions of her family:

> So much of anxiety, care and sorrow, just for me and my future!! Why are the thoughts of Indian parents so different! . . . Many of them don't think of their happiness. They try to fulfill their dreams

> through their children's lives. Why? Don't they think about what will happen to their children's dreams!? (*Ibid.*, 157)

The first generation is overprotective about the second in many ways. This suggests that there has been little or no change in the attitude of Indian immigrants in the fast-paced land, America. Parent-child relationships are the most pressing issue confronting the Indian community today in the United States. Parents do not seem to understand the influence of the social environment on their children. The school system, television, as well as their peer group may influence second-generation Indian Americans in many ways that the parents are unaware of and they still persist on maintaining their own customs.

Soma Sudeshana Reddy has brought out very intensely the controversial mentalities of the first and second generation. The conversations between the characters picture the Indian immigrants and their problems of survival. Parents in general do worry about their children's future, especially when the children are daughters. Girls are under a stricter surveillance than boys, for it is felt that too much freedom might spoil a girl's reputation and thus damage her chances of going for a good marriage.

In addition, the status and prestige of the family as a whole depends upon keeping its reputation, much of which rests on the chaste behaviour of the women. For Indians who immigrated to far off lands, raising their children is a difficult task. Janaki's trial in bringing up her daughters, protecting them from the American culture and inculcating their own customs and traditions, gives a telling description of the concern of an Indian parent for her children. The author has constructed the story using apt images to bring out different attitudes of the parents and the children: "Mom, you come and take the bag. I want to eat onion 'pakoras' dipped in hot fudge" (*Ibid.*, 161-62).

The imagery of "onion pakora", an Indian food mixed with "hot fudge" an American, is not merely the food that she wants to eat but replicates the trial of the daughter trying to unite two cultures. This shows how the second generation cannot leave its past culture though it is influenced by the western atmosphere. The author proves that the second generation is not carried away completely by alien traditions. In general, while the second generation is Americanized with the influence of school friends and the society around them, it is also strongly influenced by its parents' tradition and religion. They may listen to pop music and watch American movies, but they are also comfortable with the classical music and Indian movies. They also have a tendency to follow their parents' wish when it comes to issues like marriage and child-bearing.

"Passing Phase" from *Proceedings of Fourth International Telugu Conference* is another story written by Soma Sudeshana Reddy. The author depicts the changing phases in a person's life. At any point of time in life, there are conflicts between parents and children. The author represents that they exist more in diasporic Indian families due to the heavy pressure they experience from inside and outside.

Cultural differences remain in the host country cultivated from the home country. The impact of the host community, particularly the outside environment is more profound than that of the family. This is what Sangeetha, born and brought up in America, experiences:

> Sangeetha is an American girl born in an Indian family. She was acclimatized to the American life although she was accustomed to Indian traditions and Indian food. (Reddy, "Passing Phase" 130)

Being born in America, Sangeetha looks at herself as a citizen of the United States and is more inclined to the American way of life than to the Indian one. In fact, the second-generation children have to adjust properly to and assimilate with the American way of life so as to be fully accepted by the host country.

The author proves that the American-born generation cannot be a replica of the parents. Developing an Indian identity is based on immigrants' memories of a homeland and the sense of isolation that they feel in the United States:

> Once upon a time when children conversed with their parents, they used to think and talk. These days though parents think and decide and try to talk slowly, there is no use. In this country that word is like a powerful generation breaking through the depths of the universe to a different world. (*Ibid.*, 130)

The sentimental attachment for India is, of course, very little for those who have not grown up in India, thus creating a doubt as to whether the American-born generation can really possess the ability to develop a strong Indian life. In this sense, the difference between Indian immigrants and American-born Indians is based less on a generation gap and more on the role that the memory of India plays in defining the social relationship and the relationship between parents and children.

The fear of their culture being detested by their children is so intense that parents sometimes resort to understand the needs and apply measures to safeguard it at the same time giving importance to the kids' requirements:

> That age is different. Their desires are different. We should remind them sometimes of the fencing. Sometimes we should open the fencing and let them go. (*Ibid.*, 131)

During some of my interviews, when conversing about the preservation of culture, the father of a child agreed that times have changed. He said that being an Indian was different for him than for his children. He said he could not force them to do things according to his wish but he could only hope that they would be able to maintain some of "our" culture.

The use of the word "our" culture rather than "my" culture refers to a family identity, rather than an individual identity. This statement suggests a growing acceptance of their children's westernization. The issue of "freedom", the American value for which many parents immigrated to the United States, tends to indicate a conflict between the cultures they have inherited and the one they belong to.

Apart from this, Tanmayi as a typical Indian mother fears the westernized atmosphere around Sangeetha:

> Desire for sexual liaison should be with your husband after marriage. Whoever follows the Hindu faith will believe in this. Try to understand. (*Ibid.*, 131)

In general it is accepted that housework is woman's work, and that girls need protection so that their virginity is safeguarded by preventing sexual relations outside marriage. As future women, it is assumed that they have to make sure that ethnic culture is transmitted from one generation to the next. This requires that girls participate to a greater extent in cultural and religious activities.

Sangeetha is troubled by the statement that girls need to be overprotected and boys were given the freedom to choose their own style:

> There are no such restrictions to the Indian boys. They have the luck of dating . . . we should hide our desires till our marriage, then start life with half-dead enthusiasm. We should lead a life of compromise like our Indian parents . . . isn't it? (*Ibid.*, 131)

However, for the most part, such arguments continue to take place within the framework of shared values. Most young Indian girls try to avoid open conflict with their parents, not so much because they are physically afraid of them, but because they feel that they ought to obey their parents and avoid dishonouring the family. In general, boys are also expected to learn their mother tongue and marry within the ethnic community. But boys can date for fun, and experiment with life to some extent as long as they retain their ethnic culture. But, as boys become teenagers, they tend to break away from the family hold, while girls experience a tight grip.

Sangeetha too experiences the same with her parents who belong to the conservative traditions and culture. She experiences the trauma, struggling between two customs unable to imbibe either one of them. Tanmayi remains conventional, like many others who believe in maintaining the customs as a part of their heritage, and hopes that their children will also be able to incorporate the best of both cultures.

All my second-generation respondents have stated that their parents work very hard and go out of their way to ensure that their children study well and achieve the goal of having successful careers. Being an Indian American is different, because one is always better than average. The parents, who immigrated primarily in search of better opportunities, put a high premium on economic success. In general, parents are partial to their ethnic cultural heritage and are very desirous of preserving and transmitting it to the second generation. They do face conflict with their children in this endeavour and are ready to make compromises to maintain harmony between the two generations. But there are definite limits with regard to the kind of compromises they are ready to make. This is reflected in Chitra Banerjee Divakaruni's "Doors" in *Arranged Marriage*.

Preeti was born in India but has migrated to the United States at the age of six. Thus her upbringing is of a second-generation immigrant and she wishes to marry Deepak, a first-generation immigrant in the story. Preeti's mother warns her to be careful because she herself as a first-generation immigrant experiences the problem of adjustment between two different cultures and traditions:

> Here you are, living in the U.S. . . . And Deepak—he's straight out of India. Just because you took a few classes together at the University, and you liked how he talks, doesn't mean that you can live with him. (Divakaruni, "Doors" 183)

Parents do want to help their children integrate into the larger society. But first-generation immigrants fear that their ethnic culture is devalued in the larger society. The second generation is not always of the same view and there arises some degree of conflict with their parents. Second-generation immigrants are aware throughout their childhood and adolescence that their parents intend to arrange a marriage for them. Many of the arguments between children and their parents are not so much about the choice of a spouse or the style of the wedding, but about the wider consequences of conformity.

Preeti's mother worries about her daughter's future in trying to balance two different customs:

> "It's never too late to stop yourself from ruining your life," her mother said. "What do you *really* know about how Indian men think? About what they expect from their women?" (*Ibid.*, 184)

On a few occasions, the second generation fights against the rules and high expectations that the first generation imposes upon it. While these conflicts appear on the surface to be a normal parent-child clash, they are perceived differently because of cultural differences:

> "*That's* your problem!" Preeti's mother flared. "Making a joke of everything, thinking the world will always let you have your own way. I wish I *had* trained you better, like my mother did me, to be obedient and adjusting and forgiving. You're going to need it." (*Ibid.*, 184)

There are occasions when the parents feel insecure about raising their children. There are definitely situations when they repent their status: "'They were all brought up here, like you.' Her mother refused to be charmed. 'Not with a set of pre historic values'" (Divakaruni, "Doors" 184). We find the parents at times feeling guilty in forcing their children to follow the traditions. This sense of guilt among the second generation is a powerful motivator for family loyalty and development of a collective identity.

The second generation is termed "ABCD" meaning 'American Born Confused Desis'. Many of the second generation are indeed confused between two worlds: "It's no wonder we call them ABCDs . . . American born confused Desis." (Divakaruni, "Doors" 185). As strangers in a strange land, Indians are confronted with conflicts between their traditional culture and American culture. These conflicts induce an identity crisis even as immigrants and their children strive to find a balance.

"Meeting Mrinal" from *Arranged Marriage* by Chitra Banerjee Divakaruni replicates the character of an Indian woman playing the dual role of being a wife to an Americanized husband and a mother to an American-born son Dinesh, who prefers to be addressed as Dean. Having shorter American sounding names seems like a way to maintain an Indian identity while also adapting to American culture. Divakaruni uses names for her characters to signal the changes in cultural identity and, by implication, diasporic consciousness: "A moment later Dean, as my teenage son Dinesh prefers to be addressed, sauntered into the kitchen" (Divakaruni, "Meeting Mrinal" 273).

There seems to be a suggestion that if the child has an American or American-sounding name, it is more likely that the child is born in the United States. Names in India are very important because usually the name can indicate the person's caste, and region of origin. Here we see Asha worried with the transformation of her son including his Americanized name. Parents are able to see beyond the use of Indian names or citizenship in defining their own or their children's identity:

> Recently when I think of Dinesh I have a sinking feeling inside me. I tell myself that I shouldn't be too concerned about his clothing or hairstyle, or even the long hours when he shuts himself up in his room and listens to music that sounds furious. (Divakaruni, "Meeting Mrinal" 276)

Some of them think that they will be more understanding and accommodating towards their own children. They think that they will put fewer restrictions and hear the children's point of view. They try to be more open with children so as to make their lives more free and relaxed. Asha, who wishes to direct her son into traditional ways, keeps her interests to her own self, realizing the needs of her son. The role of the parents in taking care of their children plays a major part in Indian families:

> "Why don't you move to an apartment, Asha", my supervisor keeps telling me. "It'd be a lot cheaper and you wouldn't have to fight the memories." She's right. But Dinesh has lived in this house all his life. I feel that if I can hold on to it until he graduates, a year longer. (*Ibid.*, 277)

Here we see the trouble Asha faces to create some comfort to Dinesh. The sense of sacrifice appears common among Indian parents. They sacrifice their interests and almost their entire lives to make their children happy. In this story, we find the mother struggling alone to face grave situations while the husband is depicted as a coward who elopes leaving his wife and his son. Asha, in the role of a mother and a father, stands firm to protect her son and succeeds towards the end.

At every stage, she tries to raise Dinesh in a traditional way, allowing for a touch of western impact when needed. She induces in him the respect for elders:

> He imitated my Indian accent, thickening it in exaggeration. "Why couldn't you just tell her the fucking truth—that he got tired of you and left you for another woman." That's when I slapped him. (*Ibid.*, 283)

Children born in the United States seem to adjust to American culture more readily than their immigrant parents, thus creating a conflict especially in issues such as relationship with the opposite sex and social values. This is a major source of stress between the parents and their children.

We notice the mother correcting her grown-up son for raising his voice against his father. As children begin to learn to question things, they often are viewed as being disrespectful. Often the second generation hears the parents say, "I was never allowed to speak to my parents that way." Conflict can therefore arise when some Indian families try to embrace the western concept of freedom while at the same time maintaining a collective family identity. The author in "Meeting Mrinal" tries to balance both the traditions in her two characters, the mother and the son, giving equal importance to both of them.

Diasporic women's ties of affinity to their non-western culture reinforce the mother's subordination and a sense of alienation in the west. Also central in Divakaruni's narratives is her portrayal of diasporic women resisting patriarchal control and articulating the sense of the self. Thus, she suggests that the process of self-definition often entails recognition of cultural and social ties of affinity that manifest diasporic consciousness.

Secondly, we see Dinesh changed and adapted to the tradition of his mother, as deeply-held feelings, and loyalty to his family are reinforced in his response to rejection from outside. Generally, the second generation moves confidently in both the Indian and American spaces but the majority continue to feel that their roots are in Indian culture. They are seeking to reform and modify their parents' values, rather than to move away from them completely. Thus we visualize the characters struggling in the west to impart their own culture and finally succeeding in this respect.

"I Want to Give You Devotion" from *Contours of the Heart* is a story written by Ameena Meer.[4] Ameena Meer is an Indian, living and writing in New York City. Her journalistic writings have appeared in *Harper's Bazaar* and *Interview and Spin*. Her short fiction has been anthologized in *The Flaming Spirit*, *New Writing 3: New British and Commonwealth Writing*, and *On a Bed of Rice*, and her first novel is *Bombay Talkies*.

This is the story of contradiction between the first and the second generation. It is the story of Anu who gets frustrated with two customs, unable to imbibe either of them. Anu visits India at the age of five. When she returns back to America she narrates her views on India and its culture to her classmates and this incident gives us an idea of how a girl of Indian origin born and brought up in America perceives her own land:

> I said, "It's really hot. You just go outside for five minutes and you have to come back in and have a bath and change your clothes." I said, "I changed all my clothes three times a day. I remembered the colour of the sunlight . . . cows walk around all over the place. There are animals everywhere." (Meer, "I Want to Give You Devotion" 94)

The second generation participates in the American educational system and is exposed to the values of its American friends. A gulf between second-generation immigrants and their parents is inevitable, but it is usually not so wide or so clear-cut as outsiders may assume. Second-generation immigrants have a poor opinion of their own land. For the children, ever since their early years, right and wrong, good and bad are all tangled in what is Indian and what is American. The western impact leaves them with a despicable impression on their motherland. The process of adaptation assumes at least minimal changes in identity with the immigrant group: "I was just an ordinary kid there, so I laughed too. Anyway, I wasn't a very popular child. Not unpopular either. But nothing special" (*Ibid*., 94).

It is not quite enough even when ethnic families do their best to assure their children of their intrinsic self-worth. Children have to spend a considerable part of their daily life in schools and among their friends. The realization that they are different are devalued for that reason hurts especially when there is not much the child can do to change the situation.

Ameena Meer's story brings out certain incidents, where second-generation children struggle between two cultures, and feel very difficult to stay in traditional conservative families absorbing themselves into the fast culture of America. Even the parents undergo problems in trying to adjust them to two different traditions. Especially, when woman takes an initiative to raise her children, keeping aside her own interests:

> My mother, like all good Indian mothers, made sure that I am well-protected. Despite all her modern trappings, she couldn't keep from wanting to safeguard her daughters' reputations as well as our chastity. We were always carefully observed and—while every whim was indulged—we were sheltered from any of life's harsh realities. (*Ibid.*, 101)

American family life is also puzzling and threatening for many Indian parents. It seems insecure and there appears to be little respect for older generation. Marriages break up, old people go into homes and children into day care for what seems to be the flimsiest of reasons, and sexual license is visible everywhere. Such behaviour is inhuman and outrageous according to Indian standards. Ameena Meer proves through the story that the second generation does suffer between two spaces, one they belong to which they have left and the other, a promising one. But one needs to make a right decision to pick up the good things and follow the correct one. Anu succeeds in organizing her life with the help of her mother.

This chapter has shown how western culture becomes a source of conflict for parents who realize that their children are just as much Americans as they are Indians and therefore they cannot be forced into the traditional ways of India. But some parents also perceive different ways of living and maintain the values that are important, regardless of what is being done in India. Thus, parents are able to see the generation gap between the way they were raised and the way things are currently happening in both the United States and India.

Literary stories on the second-generation Indian-Americans are sparse. Even though many stories elaborate on the parental expectations of children, there are very few stories that deal with children's expectations of themselves. The few that are available indicate that the concerns and preoccupations of two generations are not always the same and there is at least some degree of conflict with the parents. The overwhelming concern among these young people is to be accepted as legitimate members of American society with all the rights and duties that it entails. Most of them are of the opinion that they do not belong in the American social milieu. Under such circumstances, they are trying to do their best to organize their lives. Obviously, the strategies they adopt are different.

Culture is the background, taken for granted and problematic all of which we ourselves have constructed. Often these social constructions take on a life of their own in producing culture-making institutions. It is used to structure and organize the environment. It helps in times of conflict and crisis to guide one through the problems, as well as to see the world and to interact with others. From these women writers, we learn that women's diasporic consciousness involves diasporic women's social affiliations. It also involves diasporic women's awareness of the possibility of emancipation from patriarchal structures and the possibility of self-definition.

Growing up in an Indian family in the United States does not in itself cause stress. Many of the problems which do occur are not the result of conflicts caused by migration and the experience of great social change, but of external pressures. Living in inner city areas, where they have poor facilities can also give rise to tension and anxiety which are compounded by racial hostility. The writers writing in Telugu and English deal with the same complexities that are imposed on motherhood. There are similarities in the way they deal with the concept of the first and second generation.

Most of the stories we have discussed deal with the mother playing a more prominent role in taking care of the children than the father who is involved in his social life. It is not that fathers do not take an initiative but mostly it is the mother who faces the responsibility for father is viewed as a breadwinner. I am dealing with women writers who concentrate on sensitive issues like marital relations, children and culture. If these issues are dealt with by the male writers they would not have as much emotion and not have been as explicit as the women writers. While dealing with motherhood, women writers look at its complexities very intensely.

I have concentrated only on the first-generation writers to analyse my arguments for to my knowledge there are no second-generation writers writing in Telugu. Therefore their views in dealing with this conflict are not available to us. But we have second-generation writers who are writing in English, among whom Jhumpa Lahiri can be taken into account. I have stated her to be a second-generation writer though born in England and migrated to the United States at the age of three for she considers herself to be an "American born." Jhumpa Lahiri is different from other Indian writers writing in English. She writes about Indians who have settled either in the United States of America or England.

Asian Indian children, like most second-generation Americans, are straddling across two cultures. While they are as Americanized as their schoolmates, they are strongly influenced by their parents' tradition and religion. They may listen to American pop music and watch American movies, but they are also comfortable with the popular music and movies from India. They also tend to follow the ways of their parents. This dual existence has brought out the complexities of the subculture. The next chapter addresses some of these complexities.

NOTES

1. The title is an acronym of the original for "America Bharatiya Suthulu and America Bharatiya Thallithandrulu"
2. My reading here is based on Anwar's *Between Cultures* and Varma and Seshan's *Fractured Identity*.

3. This reading is based on Fisher's *The Indians of New York City.*
4. Ameena Meer is an Indian born in Boston but most part of her education was done in India. Thus I term her as a first-generation writer for she talks of the conflict between the first and second generation in this story. Here she can be looked as playing a dual role, one as a first-generation writer acquainted with Indian traditions and the other as a second-generation writer for being an American born.

Chapter 4

"Khichri" Identities: Caste, Religion and Culture

The history of Indians migrating to many parts of the world is a phenomenon which has been a subject of study for quite some time. Apparently traditional ways of life, close family ties, and the persistence of Indian culture have been the characteristics of Indian immigrant population. In fact, cultural identity for the Indians has two significant components, one religious and the other having to do with daily routine.

The renowned scholar Stuart Hall in "Cultural Identity and Representation" in J. Rutherford's edited text, *Identity: Community, Culture, Difference* remarks that "[w]e all write and speak from a particular place and time, from a history and a culture which is specific. What we say is always 'in context' positioned" (222). Hall's statement is a useful reminder that immigrants' experiences and their very lives are shaped by the social location. Their history, their culture, their geographical location, as well as other elements go into the formation of their cultural identities.

The present chapter is a study on issues that are acquiring increasing relevance in the modern world—namely, caste, religion and traditional culture. It attempts to see how the immigrants maintain and sustain their cultural identities. The potential uses of media for such purposes are also explored. Culture is more than a shared taste or preference. Culture on the whole makes two kinds of impact on its adherents. On one hand, it endows certain activities and experiences with some values, but on the other it imposes certain constraints. These constraints can be either direct or indirect.

Many societies around the world have become increasingly multicultural in nature during the past decade. One of the reasons for this is the migration of people from one country to another. Most often it is found that people from developing countries migrate to developed countries. These migrants are mostly scientists, engineers, doctors, nurses, teachers and writers. Ultimately, what happens to these migrants? Are they accepted in the countries of their domicile? Do they achieve their goals of migration? These questions are reflected in most of the writings of the immigrants.

Cultural identity is formed through an interaction of tradition, history, spiritual and societal values. And tradition is a link between the past and the present and involves an active display of the questions of approval and disapproval. With more and more writers of Indian origin settling abroad and engaging themselves in creative writing, it is important to consider what parameters ought to be used to judge their works. Research-based studies[1] in literature indicate that varying styles are used in the literature of the diaspora and they are dependent on the migrant status of Indians in America and their links with Indian culture.

Significantly, people have recognized Indian writing in English, no matter where it comes from. It is really interesting that a great deal of Indian writing in English is known to be produced in different parts of the world. But very little is known about regional writing, especially, Indian writing in Telugu and its status abroad. No research-based evidence is found, as there is very little concern for Telugu writing in the United States. This chapter is based on such concern, to peep into the life of the Indian migrants through the writings of Indian women writers, writing in Telugu and English. This chapter deals with the reflection of culture in their writings and the way the writers deal with the concept in terms of both an Indian and a regional identity.

This is a brief exploratory study of how Indian immigrants in the United States form a new identity, while maintaining the notion of traditional culture. Indians are a mixture of many divergent cultures held together by the Gandhian dream of unity and self-rule. They have a rich cultural heritage, which is often ignored by people having a western fixation. This chapter explores the concepts of culture, identity and the process of identity formation among immigrants. In the recent years, a great body of fiction has emerged on the world literary scene written by writers of Indian origin. A large number of these diasporic writers have given expression to their creative urge and have brought credit to diasporic fiction as a distinctive force.

Chimata Kamala's "America Illaalu" (American Housewife) from *America Telugu Katha* is a story about an immigrant Indian wife and her problems in adjusting to the fast-paced land. Chimata Kamala lives in Chicago and writes poetry, fiction and drama and is greatly interested in Telugu literature and fine arts. The story begins with the festival of Ganesh Chaturthi which Indians celebrate with great splendour. In order to keep up her past traditions and culture, the protagonist wishes to include it in the busy schedule of her daily life:

> In the beginning, I would wake up the children early to perform services to God. Later this had stopped. Now-a-days family worship is scheduled for every weekend. In America, God has got adjusted to the circumstances . . . we all disperse after the children recite the *mantra-pushpam*. (Kamala, "America Illaalu" 77-78)

When people migrate from one region to another, they find themselves in a completely different culture and that is why they take some time to settle down and assimilate the culture there. Indian immigrants gather together to perform group worship. It is viewed as an important means of transferring culture and values. Some Indian women in America, though unaware of the rituals, make an effort to study and practise them in their house. It is so because they do not want to leave their culture behind and they want their children to grow up with their traditional culture. Likewise, maintaining rituals is viewed as a family responsibility rather than an individual one.

We find the protagonist of the story struggling between two cultures and her discontent with the American life:

> Though living in a great nation, a mysterious kind of dissatisfaction. . . . The dilemma is not understanding the original problem. . . . I am not sure if I have taken a wrong step or a right one of coming to this country. (*Ibid.*, 79)

Like many immigrants, the protagonist finds it difficult to adjust to the new world and new customs and to leave her past behind. Towards the end she says that she is unable to behave either like an Indian wife or like an American caught between two worlds:

> I am unable to be like a full-fledged Indian wife nor could I convert myself into an American housewife. I am none other than "American Housewife" hanging in the third heaven. (*Ibid.*, 79)

Generally, for both women living in India and those who have immigrated, employment brings more pain than pleasure. Thus, the present story portrays the difficulties faced by an Indian wife in an alien atmosphere, without friends or relatives, struggling to cope with the new surroundings she cannot call her "home." She has problems in maintaining rituals connected with the festival, for her office work and the necessity to drink wine in the office party demand that she be modern. Wondering whether it is accurate to drink wine on a festive day, she approaches her best friend, the computer, which replicates her life as a motorized one:

> If it is dinner, they serve wine too! I don't know if I can drink wine on the day of *puja*? . . . The ever-present God who has answers to all the questions in the world on its finger tips. My best friend. It's better if I ask my computer. (*Ibid.*, 79)

The representation of the protagonist approaching the computer portrays her life as a mechanical one. This also indicates her status as a lonely person with no friend to share her emotions. This can be compared to Chitra Banerjee Divakaruni's poem "We the Indian Women in America", from Sunaina Maira and Rajini Srikanth's edited book, *Contours of the Heart*, where the Indian women in America are caught between two worlds supervising both their families and their workplaces and still unable to justify either of them:

> It's not always easy for us, Indian women in America. We came with dreams of instant riches, . . . but slowly we learned being alone is not all bad. . . . And what we want is this: for us and our daughters, Indian and American, the best of both together. (Divakaruni, "We the Indian Women in America" 260-61)

This justifies that immigrant women in general are neither completely Indian nor western. They stand halfway between the identities, failing to substantiate either of them. The poet, as an immigrant Indian woman, reproduces herself in the character of the story. Chimata Kamala too plays the two roles, an earning member in the family and also pictures herself as an "American Housewife." The author may have also faced similar problems in adjusting to both the worlds, living in a country where she did not have her kith or kin to share her emotions, as depicted in the story. This title is quite apt in discussing the responsibilities of a "wife" in America. The author points out the dilemma of an immigrant woman trying to bring together the culture she lives in, and the one she comes from.

Soma Sudeshana Reddy is another writer who concentrates on the concept of culture and cultural identity. Her short story "Mogudu Kavaala" (Want a Husband) from *America Telugu Katha* supports her argument that religion plays a vital role in the lives of Indian families. Religious affiliations keep many migrants well-linked to their places of origin, especially as a large number are still first-generation immigrants. The story proves that religious beliefs and traditional superstitions persist in the immigrants though they stay in America.

> "Let your daughter perform the 'andaalu' penance. If it is not possible for her . . . ask her to keep a small idol in a ziplock bag and tell her to keep it under her pillow. Let's hope that the time will arrive fast as a rocket" she said. (Reddy, "Mogudu Kavaala" 158-59)

Some Indian women in America make it a point to study and practise the rituals. It is so because they do not want to leave their culture behind and want their children to grow up in their traditional culture:

> During that time of worship, an auspicious moment will come, at that moment the three core deities will cast their glance at us for a minute, the worship offered at that moment will be fulfilled, and such a moment will come only once in a century." . . . Seema smiled thinking that her mother's modern ideas are slipping away. (*Ibid.*, 159)

Janaki's act of arranging an old customary puja (prayer) in a foreign land confirms that Indians, though living in an alien land, do give importance to their religious beliefs. This short story supports the hypothesis that religiosity among Indian immigrants has not declined as a result of immigration. On the contrary, there is greater religious consciousness and a need to practise some religious rituals individually as well as communally:

> "Seema will you get that ziplock bag under your pillow." "Why mummy! The one you have given me that day . . ." Though she laughed that day, she has got sentimental over it now. "Siri will be a graduate next year! I want to keep it under her pillow." (*Ibid.*, 161)

The important thing to note about culture is the way it is imbibed. Culture is something that is passed on from generation to generation, and human beings acquire it within a social context. The process of acquiring culture begins at birth, as individuals adapt to the norms of social behaviour prescribed by society. They start assimilating the complex cultural codes that provide meaning for that particular society.

Soma Sudeshana Reddy also uses images to support her arguments in the story:

> After watching the movie when he went to drop Seema, she invited him inside. He was a bit shy. When he entered the house, he started petting the dog that jumped on him. (*Ibid.*, 160)

Petting the dog signifies his acceptance of Seema and her culture. Through this character, the author fulfills Janaki's wish to see her daughter married and her longstanding beliefs of giving importance to their caste, religion and culture. Religion has always been at the core of the Indian way of life. According to Petty's Gregory Lee, religious identity maintains its traditional tolerance in a variety of ways. Among the immigrant groups, religious practice tends to be a mode of education, with its being passed from generation to generation.

My study of this story clearly suggests that there are marked differences between the attitudes of those who have children and those who do not. Those with children have a more favourable attitude toward religion and religious practices, since they see these as a way of raising Indian consciousness among their children. In order to bring up children according to Indian traditions, participation in religious practices becomes important.

Pattisapu Radha Mahalakshmi's "Smoky Mountains" in *America Telugu Kathanika* is a story that exposes the life of the protagonist who undergoes many pressures in all the phases of her life. The author speaks about the existing value system in Indian families. She tries to concentrate on all the issues that diasporic Indian families face in an alien land. One interesting thing in the story is the aspect of caste and religion. Almost all the stories that we have read deal with the concept of religion. But they have never mentioned the caste system.

Most of the writers writing in English have talked about being a "Hindu" while living in a Christian land, America. There have been many instances where the white men point at Indians and say "Hindus." It is so because, normally Indians are associated with their Hindu religion and the language they speak. For Americans, if you are from India you are a Hindu. In Bharati Mukherjee's short story "Hindus" in *Darkness*, Lisa, an American, points at the protagonist and says,

> "I had no idea you spoke Hindu." . . . "I speak Hindu. No matter what language I speak it will come out slightly foreign, no matter how perfectly I mouth it. There's a whole world of us now, speaking Hindu." (Mukherjee, "Hindus" 140)

The writers in general distinguish Indians from Americans in terms of religion. But they never talk about the caste system. "Smoky Mountains" is quite interesting as the author Pattisapu Radha Mahalakshmi writes about the theme of caste as a primary reference. The protagonist, Meenakshi, accidentally meets Narahari, a tourist, in a hotel in "Smoky Mountains":

> "The way you have tied a white saree . . . at first I thought you were a nun. So you are a baby sitter." He said. "I am Narahari. My wife died long time back. I have a eleven year old son. We are Brahmins," he replied again. (Mahalakshmi, "Smoky Mountains" 68)

Here the conversation between Narahari and Meenakshi gives us a picture of two strangers conversing for the first time. Normally back in India and especially in Andhra Pradesh when two elderly strangers meet for the first time, each of them shows curiosity to know every minute detail of the other person, including her/his caste and religion. But in America talking about religion is itself a great achievement. Thus, no writer in English dealt in this book makes an effort to bring out the concept of caste. They talk about being an Indian in an alien land, being a Hindu in a Christian land. But difference in expression when related with these sensitive terms is noticed in the writers writing in Telugu:

> "I am Meenakshi. I lost my husband, when I was very young, maybe when I was around eleven or twelve years. We are Brahmins." Then a sudden thought occurred in Narahari's mind. Instead

> of looking out for a babysitter why not look out for a wife. (*Ibid.*, 68)

Thus, the internal connotation of the author dealing with the question of caste is made apparent to the reader. Once Narahari recognizes that Meenakshi is a Brahmin like him, he wishes to marry her at the very first instance which of course looks very hasty. This gives a clear vision of Indian immigrants still clinging on to the caste system and ethnicity. Earlier, the diasporic writers have portrayed the immigrants travel to an alien society. Later, they have talked about the immigrants undergoing different phases in a fantasy land. Now the writers have reached a stage of discussing sensitive factors as the caste system in a land where such questions had never risen before.

There are also other short stories that discuss the concept of caste and its importance, but in an indirect manner. While we move forward, this chapter discusses about the expression of caste in some of the conversations. For example, we will look at these characteristics in Puccha Annapurna's "Pelli" where the mother insists on the necessity of her daughter getting married to a man from the same caste, religion and culture. Their conversations highlight their notion of upper class, upper caste culture. There are men writers writing in America using these terms directly but humorously to alleviate the reader's mind set. The best example we could use to show how caste is significant is to see how Telugu organizations in the United States are based on caste groups. Though they contradict the truth in this, it is observed by the whole community that they are based on caste, which definitely supports our argument.

The arguments can also be linked to Mahalakshmi's background, the place she has hailed from and the new environment she stays in living with her children. One of the reasons might be that her perception of America is different in experience when compared to that of her children. For unlike most of our first-generation immigrants it is the author, who reared and looked after her children in America, but it is the children who take care of their mother and in particular my personal interaction with her in Boston supports my statement. She is a woman who always looks back at India and most of her short stories reflect her experiences back in India. She does not care about criticizing America strongly because she is confident that she does not need money or critical acclaim in America. She just wants to spread Hindu traditions and culture to the diasporic people around her. Therefore, I feel the need to look at the short stories from the author's perspective.

"Namarupaalu" (Identity) is a short story from Chimata Kamala's collection, *America Illaalu,* where she describes the fear of losing their culture and tradition in every aspect, including their names. The whole story is based on how names are being changed in western society in order to make them sound American. All through the story she praises Indian names and the importance Indians bestow upon them. She says names in India are very important:

> Of course, everything was haywire when I came to America. First name became last and last the first. Sometimes the names lost their head and tail and became a two letter word. The popular Andhra name "Subbarao" usually changed gender and became an American "Subha." Would you believe this!! (Kamala, "Namarupaalu" 52)

Many immigrants change their original names to ease the pronunciation. Most often they use their initials. This tells us how the identity of the immigrant changes from the name shortened of their own accord or through a traditional name being modified to sound more American. This seems like the way they could maintain an Indian identity while also adapting to American culture. In India names are very significant, because even by the name one can determine a person's caste and the region of origin. The mode of address too is culture specific. Consider the following:

> My elder daughter born and brought up in the free American atmosphere, one day had a big argument with her grandpa. "Grandma addresses you with respect. So why don't you reciprocate in the same manner. Or else I will ask her to address you differently." She declared haughtily. (*Ibid.*, 51)

This is a beautiful quotation from the text where the reader notices the change in the second generation not accepting certain values implicitly. Back in India, women are taught and forced to obey men. They are not expected to be outspoken. But due to their immigration to the land of freedom, there is a positive change. Each generation has the choice of selecting, rejecting, modifying and adjusting to those aspects of its heritage and tradition that it deems proper:

> The world is changing. New names are coming to light. Will our names from the past brighten in the future? . . . This is just the time to find solutions. (*Ibid.*, 53)

Slowly, people are adjusting to the changing norms of American society. What is considered fundamentally important is retained and guarded, while some aspects that are considered inconsequential are altered or discarded altogether. Tradition is thus a flexible and dynamic concept which allows communities to maintain a link between the past and the present, and helps them sustain their culture.

The quotation mentioned above proves that though many fear losing their culture and tradition, they still try to adjust themselves to the circumstances. Their statements reveal that they change in their attitudes towards "American" culture and values. Consciously or unconsciously, they have begun to internalize those aspects of American culture that they feel are worth emulating. Instead of situating themselves in one culture, they have chosen a two-tiered culture that they feel best addresses their needs.

"Aasakiranam" (Ray of Hope) from *America Telugu Kathanika* is a different story by Pudipedhi Seshu Sarma compared to her other short stories. The whole story revolves around the confusion of a retired professor who visits United States of America on a conference to deliver a lecture on "diasporic Indians." His fear of Indian immigrants in America losing their language and culture is illustrated very well by the author, using rhythmic connections between passages. The author constructs the story line dealing with the protagonist's experiences and finally his acquaintance with a person that he least expects to meet:

> Grandpa Bhaskar and Grandma Sudha respect our tradition and culture just like us. Although they live in America, they built a Vinayaka temple at their place and struggled a lot to teach their children about Hindu religion. They carefully selected good families from their own caste for their four children. (Sarma, "Ray of Hope" 17)

Building temples, celebrating festivals and rituals are thus seen as affirmations of cultural identity. This is not only because one experiences a sense of history through these rituals, but also because one accepts this view implicitly. An understanding of one's origin helps in maintaining the sense of continuity. This is needed to a certain extent because it helps find a personal and social meaning of human existence:

> Keep aside being a Telugu. Either to spread Hinduism in this country or for whatever individual reason, they build one or two temples at every corner. Those who were interested in our religion or respected it offered prayers either at their homes or in the temples. (*Ibid.*, 18)

The religiosity of Indian immigrants has increased in some ways. Almost all maintain an altar at home and observe religious festivities whenever possible. This is seen as a means of maintaining cultural identity.

It seems, therefore, that the fear of the loss of Indianness has to be considered alongside the hopes of acceptance by and into American society. For the first-generation who had spent the earlier part of their lives in India, the feeling of "otherness" is also experienced through the absence of the social and cultural infrastructures that were part of their childhood and youth in India.

> Within a century, in two or three generations, our families will become as American. Nothing surprising. But other nationalities especially the Muslims and the Jews are trying to protect their cultures through succeeding generations. But what are we doing? (*Ibid.*, 18)

Here we notice the author questioning the readers through her characters in the story. The fear of loss and emptiness is evident in the above.

It is ironic to hear the respondents talk about the feeling of being the "other" in a predominantly white society and that none of them discussed the possibility of returning to India. Going back permanently was not considered a feasible proposition. The focus, rather, was on finding ways to adjust to or live with the fact of being the "other." The respondents implicitly accepted the United States as their new home. They knew that they no longer "fitted" into the Indian society that they had left behind; indeed they were not certain that they even wanted to go back. They adopted a practical and pragmatic American attitude in making the best of this new situation, and adapting to the life there.

While on one hand, the author stresses the reluctance of Indian immigrants to return back to India, on the other, she introduces a personality who loves to reconstruct the lost tradition and culture:

> Turning to the young boy Harish asked, "Who is this young fellow?"
>
> "My name is Kavuri Hari. Everyone calls me Harry", replied the young man in poor Telugu.
>
> "O boy!!. How did you learn Telugu"? exclaimed Harish surprised. (*Ibid.*, 19)

When the present generation is getting acquainted to the American society, the new generation is making an attempt to look back at their land of origin:

> For some reasons, he always wanted to learn Telugu culture, Hindu principles. . . . Harish could not believe his ears. Why so much of interest in this young fellow? This young person is a ray of hope for him who is in the dumps for he does not know where our culture is taking us in this country. (*Ibid.*, 19)

This story is completely different from the other stories as the author captures both the fear of losing the culture and, at the same moment, rebuilding it. She tries to convince the readers that the culture they fear that is lost would definitely be retained by future generations. Past traditions and culture of the Indian diaspora do not perish. These have their own charm and one day these will emerge with a bang, shining with more intensity.

"Pelli" (Marriage) by Puccha Annapurna in *America Telugu Katha* deals with concepts like marital relationships, first and second generation conflicts, religion and culture. The author carefully manages to concentrate on these major themes, justifying them at every possible opportunity. We have already looked at the first two themes and the part they play in the lives of the diasporic Indians. Now we will try to probe into the concept of culture in dealing with the author's perception.

The protagonist Sridevi is shown as a character that conciliates on everything in her life. She does not compromise out of volition but out of compulsion. From the beginning, she is prepared to adjust and forced to lead a mechanical life. She is forced to marry at an early age, migrate to the United States and change according to the western culture. We have already discussed the imagery used by the author to describe Sridevi's mechanical life. Now consider Sridevi's far away gaze:

> Though she felt a bit cold, her eyes alighted on the far away mountains which looked calm and peaceful and rising in glory above the dusky sky. (Annapurna, "Pelli" 104)

This imagery proves true in the life of Sridevi, where she predicts everything to be positive in prospect, comparing things at a distance waiting for some good to happen in future:

> Only after coming to this completely different world thirty years back did she realize the importance of her native land's customs and traditions, language and religion, and started to appreciate them. Only after settling down in a foreign land did she come to know what "faraway clouds" are. . . . She realized that her culture is great, priceless and was above all things. (*Ibid.*, 105)

In all these statements, there is self reflexivity. The comparison with American society seems to help immigrants understand and appreciate Indian values a little better. Moreover this comparative engagement is brought out in another approach. The immigrants speak about distance as a factor that helps them evaluate their Indian roots. The physical and spatial distance from India is seen as necessary to establish an effective connection with and a deeper understanding of Indian values.

Identity is not only something you feel from inside, it is also something that is bestowed upon you from outside. The immigrants while on one hand follow their own religion, tradition and culture, on the other; they give importance to western influence:

> God is God in any religion and faith. Just because you are unaccustomed to something different from your deities, rituals and mantras that doesn't mean you should degrade other Gods. . . . The other Gods, their spiritual books, rituals taught me to be patient. (*Ibid.*, 106)

Generally, the diasporic Indians embody two diverse cultures, one part lives in the United States while the other part maintains an umbilical link with certain value systems that have been inherited from an Indian past and also its present. This duality arises out of necessity, and not by choice. Sridevi's awareness to spiritual texts is a pointer in this duality:

> Other spiritual books . . . taught me to be curious . . . but they couldn't convert me to accept a son-in-law from a foreign religion and faith. (*Ibid.*, 106-7)

Notice here a comparison between Indian and American cultures. Sridevi admits that there are differences between two cultures, and recognizes things that she prefers about American society. There is no doubt about that. She adjusts to American society but not to an "American" in the family:

> He was well-educated and well-behaved . . . however she only wanted caste, country and religion in her son-in-law. . . . Is it her bad luck that she saw a different person or her inability to forego her trusted traditions? She questioned herself for the hundredth time. (*Ibid.*, 107)

The basic attitudes and values of the Asian Indian population have not changed much as a result of immigration. Especially in the context of family and religion, we find that our characters are sometimes even more traditional than their Indian counterparts. Almost all the stories reveal ways in which their identity has been influenced by American norms and values. The reason for this is that identity is not a static concept. Cultural identity in all its various dimensions can only be understood within a specific, socially constructed world.

Bharati Mukherjee is another writer in English who discusses an emotional bond that a person develops with the place he/she lives in. Her characters deal with the concept of cultural transplantation, the process of pulling themselves out of the culture they were born in, and then replanting themselves in another culture.

Sociologist, Gregory Lee Pettys in *Asian Indians in the United States: An Analysis of Identity Formation and Retention* says that immigrants need to impart American culture and that many of the immigrants come to the United States without a clear understanding of the rituals or philosophy of America. Therefore, they find that they need to read or attend special classes in order to understand this new culture. Most of Bharati Mukherjee's writings deal with the depiction of cultural confrontation between the east and the west. This is well portrayed in her short stories in the collection *Darkness*. The immigrants are found struggling with the cultural codes of both their old and new countries and indulging in a behaviour that borders on the absurd.

The story "Lady from Lucknow" points at the changing status of a woman when culturally transplanted. Nafeesa is a Muslim woman from Lucknow who marries Iqbal and immigrates to a foreign land. She develops an extra-marital affair with Dr. James Beamish, a Pakistani, and towards the end she realizes her mistake.

The story begins with an incident in Nafeesa's neighbourhood in Lucknow back in India. Husseina who stays next door to Nafeesa falls in love with a Hindu. They stay in a Muslim locality, which is very sensitive to the conventional affairs. And when Husseina's father gets to know of his daughter's love, he beats her to death:

> Her father intercepted a love note from the boy, and beat her with his leather sandals. She died soon after . . . and I pictured the dead girl's heart—rubbery squeezable organ with . . . a first swelling, then bursting and coating the floor with thick, slippery blood. (Mukherjee, "A Lady from Lucknow" 23)

Through this incident we notice the cultural conflicts in the same country, but between people of different religious identities.

There are certain problems and concerns that Indians might face during the process of acculturation. These problems are a result of western value system, which is significantly different from that of their homeland. Indian immigrants experience strong reactions on moving to an unfamiliar foreign culture and on missing their families and extended families. These actions demand continuous adjustment, resulting in stress, frustration and hopelessness. Most Indian families try to maintain their traditional patterns, but due to forces in American society, they learn to adjust. Changes in traditional family roles and expectations are inevitable, creating stress and frustration.

The cultural difference is brought back when Nafeesa has an extra-marital affair with James. When Kate Beamish, James' wife, discovers Nafeesa and James in bed, she does not react to it furiously. Her silence tortures Nafeesa with culpability:

> That half hour wait for the cab, as Kate related tales of the grandson to her distracted husband was the most painful. It came closest to what Husseina must have felt. At least her father, the Nawab *Sahib* had beaten her. (*Ibid.*, 33)

This gives us the picture of an Indian woman exposed to a new culture. Her guilt pricks her mind and points at her culture. The immigrants say that American society has had an impact on their views on marital relationships. They find themselves halfway between the traditional Indian view and the "progressive" American one. They sometimes move towards the opposite end, trying to assimilate completely to the western ways of living.

"A Father" is another story in which the author brings out the concept of religion in each and every incident through her characters. Mr. Bhowmick is a man who gives importance to his religion. It is interesting to note once again that religion and caste factors still play an important role in the lives of Indians living in the United States of America. It is also surprising to see that it is the man who could not come out of the bondage of religion and culture, unlike the other protagonists in our stories. After his shower in the morning, Mr. Bhowmick recites prayers to Kali in Sanskrit.

His wife is not in favour of this: "She was an agnostic, a believer in ambition, not grace" (Mukherjee, "Father" 60). She is always found complaining about his prayers:

> Lately she'd begun to drain him in a wholly new way. He wasn't praying, she nagged; he was shutting her out of his life. There'd be

> no peace in the house until she hid *Kali Mata* in a suitcase. (*Ibid.*, 60)

When people migrate from one region to another, they find themselves in a completely different culture and that is why they take some time to settle down and assimilate into the culture of the foreign country. The immigrants from each nation form different groups to conduct religious festivals, cultural shows, etc., and to establish their nationality in an alien country. Even then, they do not avoid Americanization; they only behave in a more ethnic manner while trying to adjust to American culture.

It is not only the prayers that he gives importance but also his superstitions. For many Indians, religion is the main basis of ethnic identity, and it also helps establish social networks and communication. But too much of anything is a nagging nuisance to everyone around. One day when Mr. Bhowmick starts off to his work, he hears his neighbour sneeze. He believes that a sneeze brings him bad luck:

> A sneeze at the start of a journey brings bad luck. . . . Be careful out there! Mr. Bhowmick could see the goddess's scarlet little tongue tip wagging at him. (*Ibid.*, 60)

He steps back into the house to avoid bad luck. This is a story of the immigrants' struggle and their incapacity to adjust themselves to the new culture. In a strange land, as strangers, Indians are confronted with the conflict between maintaining their Indian identity, tradition and customs, and being pulled by American society to assimilate into its western culture. Hence, Indians are confronted with a crisis—an identity conflict. Here we find that both the first and the second generations are caught in this duality.

The younger generation also experiences this two-fold adjustments, but in a slightly different manner. There is pressure on the children of immigrants to somehow live two lives, to embody the best of both the worlds. Parents want their children to retain many of the traditional values of Indian society. At the same time, the parents also want their children to accept the American way of life so that they can "fit in" and excel in whatever they do.

The protagonist, Leela Lahiri, is proud of her American citizenship in the story "Hindus." At the same time she is also proud of her Bengali past. The other character Maharajah Patwant Singh of Gotlah is an expatriate with a grievance against India. When Leela and Maharajah meet after two years, Maharajah relates his pain and grievance whereas Leela celebrates her re-birth in a new world.

This does not mean that Leela has left her past behind. She is found always remembering her past and adjusting to the new atmosphere she is presently in. This is a movement from expatriation to immigration. Americans think that there is no religion in India except Hinduism. So they term all Indians as Hindus. Lisa is surprised listening to a conversation between Pat and Leela in Hindi. She says that she is surprised at their language. Lisa also says that she has a feeling that all Indians are referred to as Hindus:

> I had no idea you spoke Hindu. It's eerie to think you can speak such a hard language. . . . I'd learned from Derek to be easily incensed over ignorant confusions between Hindi and Hindu . . . but then I thought, why bother? . . . There's a whole world for us now, speaking Hindu. (Mukherjee, "Hindus" 140)

While Indians struggle to understand western culture, westerners are so ignorant as not to distinguish between Hindi language and Hindu religion.

Almost all the stories reveal ways in which the immigrants' identity has been influenced by American norms and values. The reason for this is that identity is dynamic. Identity of an individual is as much a social construct, as it is an individual creation. Thus, the cultural identity of the diaspora people straddles two lived histories—that of the root culture and that of the adopted culture.

We learn from Bharati Mukherjee that women's diasporic consciousness involves diasporic women's social alienation and subordination based on their gender, race and cultural affiliations among others. It also involves diasporic women's awareness of the possibility of emancipation from patriarchal structures and the possibility of self-definition. As a result, identity is simultaneously subjective and social, and is constituted in and through culture. Indeed, culture and identity are inextricably linked.

Bharati Mukherjee's narrative traces the conflicts of westernization due to cultural displacement. In her works immigrants are caught between two countries. Generally, Bharati Mukherjee uses her protagonists' names to indicate the change in her cultural identity and, by implication, her diasporic consciousness. The dislocation in her mind from her homeland culture is a disengagement from that culture's patriarchal mores.

"Clothes" from *Arranged Marriage* by Chitra Banerjee Divakaruni is a story of an Indian woman in the United States left alone to face the greatest disaster in her life. Sumita is married to Somesh, a store keeper, in California. The name of the store sounds "risky" to Sumita. Sumita, as an Indian woman, believes in stores being named after Gods and Goddesses to bring them luck and prosperity:

> The store was called 7-*eleven.* I thought it is a strange name, exotic, risky. All the stores I knew were piously named after gods and goddesses *Ganesh Sweet House, Lakshmi Vastralaya*—for fine saris to bring the owners luck. (Divakaruni, "Clothes" 21)

Expression of an emotional relationship to the home country lies in different ways. It is not a direct, but a derived relationship. Despite an acknowledgement of the fact that they are now Americans, the women feel it is necessary to retain their Indian heritage, both as a badge of identification in a multicultural society, and as a reflection of their true selves.

Sumita migrates to New York and stays with her in-laws. She notices that the new culture had not changed the attitude of her in-laws and Sumita endures all the restrictions. She is not supposed to wear western clothes. She has to wrap a sari around her and cover her head in front of the elders. She is not allowed to address her husband by name:

> Where I must cover my head with the edge of my Japan nylon sari . . . where like a good Indian wife I must never address my husband by his name . . . my life has turned out to be no different from Deepali's or Radha's. (*Ibid.*, 25-26)

Many believe that American culture would change any person both internally and externally which is proved wrong in the story. Though Sumita dresses secretly in western outfits for Somesh, she appears in traditional clothes before the elders.

In general, women seem to have a lot of pride in their culture. Many try to follow this culture in every aspect of their life. This seems to fit in with the traditional role of women as educators of values and traditions, and men as providers. There are more external symbols to show the young women's sense of Indian identity (dressing, *bindi*, custom of settling the house in order, singing, cooking, etc.,) than there are for young men.

It is the richness of the Indian heritage with its ability to adapt to change and conflict that makes Indian culture an important dimension for study. Indians are confronted with the challenge of trying to maintain important aspects of their traditional culture, while at the same time accommodating to the American culture. When Somesh is killed in the store, friends perform all the rituals. Thus, it is clear that Indian customs and traditions are still maintained in a fast-paced land, America.

Sumita does not wish to stay in the house like most Indian widows. She envisions herself dressed in the clothes her husband gets her and imagines working in the store.

> The thought is like an unexpected, intimate gift. I tilt my chin, readying myself. . . . In the mirror a woman holds my gaze . . . she wears a blouse and skirt the colour of almonds. (*Ibid.*, 33)

Therefore, the story points out that American culture is not always viewed from a negative perspective. It can also transform the superstitious Indian culture into a rational one.

"Silver Pavements" is another story in which the protagonist, Jayanti travels to America to attend college and in this endeavour she stays with her aunt and uncle. When Jayanti sees her aunt and uncle for the first time at the airport, she does not forget to greet the elders in a traditional manner:

> I touch their feet like a good Indian girl should, though I am somewhat embarrassed. Everyone in the airport is watching us, I'm sure of it. Aunt is embarrassed too, and shifts her weight from one leg to leg. (Divakaruni, "Silver Pavements" 38)

The American culture she ventures into confuses her. Her aunt explains her all about America and its culture. Even her uncle warns her that America is just a dream and it is not easy to cope with its culture and people:

> The Americans hate us. They're always putting us down because we're dark skinned foreigners, "*kala admi*!" Blaming us for the damn economy, for taking away their jobs. You'll see it for yourself soon enough. (*Ibid.*, 43)

His speech reveals that there are vast cultural differences between the two countries, there is heavy discrimination in employment, there is no social life, and there are only low profile jobs available for Indians and most of the good posts are reserved for the whites. He also relates the experiences he has faced in America. He says that America is a fantasy world, full of colours but when one enters it, it is nothing but blank space:

> Grief scrapes his voice. "This damn country, like a *dain*, a witch it pretends to give and then snatches everything back." (Divakaruni, "Silver Pavements" 54)

This is what the author concludes in the story—that everything in America is a dream and no person has succeeded in becoming an American. Here we notice diversified statements in two different stories by the author. In one story she praises America for converting a timid woman into a bold one and in another she blames America mentioning it as a bare land where immigrants can never find a space to fit into. This proves that one who migrates should grab the best from both the worlds and leave the bad.

In order to understand Indian life and identity, we must analyze the meaning of life for Indians. Indians are a mixture of many divergent cultures. The stories we have so far discussed offer a wonderful variety of experiences gathered from divergent cultural clashes. Immigrants feel the anxiety despite their best efforts to beat the Americans in dress and modes of behaviour. All the time, there is a feeling of being alienated. This is so because they cannot cut off the bond that ties them with their homeland.

Anuradha M. Mitra's "Romantic Stereotypes" in *Contours of the Heart* is the story of a husband and wife using a new process to maintain their tradition and culture. This is a story in the form of letters, Rahul writing to his wife Sunila, and Sunila writing to her aunt. Rahul, an immigrant in the United States writes back to his wife who is about to migrate to America. Sunila is portrayed as one waiting to be accepted into American life, whereas Rahul is seen as the one who has adjusted to American life. He writes about the difficulties of being a non-white in white American society. He says that he is unrelated to the fast-paced world.

The use of images like "*khichri*" can be viewed in terms of the emotions of the immigrants. Rahul says that he is like "*khichri*", which is a mixture of all the ingredients, dal, rice and vegetables. This exemplifies that being an immigrant is like being a mixture of all customs, adapting to the new ones and remaining tied to the past. In the same way, Rahul adjusts according to the changes in society, adopting the western culture and at the same time maintaining his own. He even says that his origin is like the water that gushes out from the "dal" after it is cleaned:

> I am like '*khichri*' incarnate, being indeterminately molded into whatever pot will contain my shape. My individuality lies awash in the saffron flavoured soft textures. . . . My national, racial, and ethnic identities work overtime to render me visible. Yet, they do entirely too much to conceal rather than reveal. (Mitra, "Romantic Stereotypes" 424)

This shows that once he is back in his homeland he would wash away the adapted customs and regain his original culture. He even expresses his feeling of being "low" among the whites: "I want to urge you, even at the stake of inviting pain that we are infinitely much less than what we are given to believe" (*Ibid.*, 425). In spite of all these obstacles, Rahul is viewed as a person who has accepted white American society.

The other image is that of wine. He guides his wife in the letter about her behaviour during the flight. He suggests her to accept the wine served during the flight and give less heed to people watching her having wine. It explains that, Rahul guides her to accept the new culture and traditions of the alien land though they seem different. He asks her to pay less heed to her past culture, for it will only confuse them in the world of new cultures.

In other words, he means to say that one should adjust and try to adopt the new culture though it is difficult, and not grumble about it and spoil the new taste it provides. While Rahul is shown as an example who adjusts to the alien land, Sunila is exposed as different through her letter to her aunt. All through the letter, her dissatisfaction of the land of opportunities is well depicted. She questions her aunt about the varied identities in America. She is disappointed with the life in America and faces an identity crisis:

> Is it because our sense of self is established in opposition to rather than in partnership with the rest of white or black or yellow Amer-

> ica? Is it this that makes us crumble and grow weak inside so that we become strangely inarticulate in expressing who we are? (*Ibid.*, 427)

Anuradha M. Mitra, the author, in this work brings out two contrary views of the husband and the wife. The husband is ready to accept the new land and the wife is unable to accept the alien land. The author has used excellent images to describe the status of Indians in an alien land. This is a story where the author gives preference to letters. Letters are used because they can visualize the personal feelings of people. Through letters, one directly reveals his or her inner feelings rather than a third person narrating his or her attitude. The image of "*khichri*" signifies a mixture of cultures. The ingredients mixed to give taste to the "*khichri*" are people from different regions who gather together to stay united and take the best of both lands.

While Rahul strives for his position, Sunila opposes the negation of herself. The author tries to portray the difference in men and women adapting to western culture. Generally, men are not deeply bound by traditions and customs, whereas women are not like them. They have certain sentiments about their culture. Thus, Rahul does not feel any problem in adapting to the western atmosphere. Though he has certain problems, he always tries to view the positive side of life. But Sunila who hails from a typical traditional family feels it difficult to adapt herself to western culture. She cannot see herself in white American society. She cannot even maintain her identity as an Indian Hindu. Like the protagonist in "America Illaalu" who struggles between two cultures, Sunila too like the other prime characters in the short stories is found struggling between the traditional culture and the need to adapt. Thus the author says that it is difficult for a woman to cut away her bonds with her past and adapt to a new environment.

It is clear from the discussion and analysis in this chapter that Indian immigrants in the United States would like to preserve their caste, religion and culture as they see these as integral parts of their ethnic and cultural identity. Religion and related aspects are seen as the fundamental part of their daily lives and as the core of their ethnic identity. To conclude, it is clear that religion and culture are likely to play their role in the formation of ethnic identities in Indian communities in the predictable future. These writers try to bring out the practice of their religion and to transmit them to the next generation as a vital part of their ethnic and cultural identities.

Studies[2] have shown that over a period of time Indian immigrant mothers in the United States tend to become more democratic and less dominant with their children. Children born in the United States seem to adjust to its culture more readily than their immigrant parents, thus creating conflicts with their parents over issues such as relationship with the opposite sex and social values. In general, there is a lot of tension between parents and their first-generation children. Asian Indians face widespread prejudice and discrimination in American society.

Due to fear of humiliation and racial discrimination, many Indians and their families discourage social contacts outside their group. Thus, many feel isolated and feel they are treated unfairly due to their country of origin, religion, and skin colour by other American citizens. Some factors, such as difficulty in communicating with others due to language barrier, speaking with an accent, style of dress, and physical appearance, contribute to the non-acceptance of Indians into the dominant American culture. To escape from stress, Indians seek support and understanding in their own community.

Many of the short stories we have studied have mentioned that Indians have become more culture conscious after coming to America, where for the first time they have had to think about the meaning of their religion and their cultural identity, something they took for granted while in India. There is a common tendency that we strive for things that we are away from. We have noticed in many short stories that most of the immigrants are more rigid and cautious in maintaining their culture after moving away from it. For example the literary gatherings and cultural meets in America prove their trial in laying a foundation for the future generations to remind them of their roots. Many attend these cultural and literary meets in order to be amongst their own people and celebrate their customs in transferring them to the upcoming generations.

We have discussed this concept of culture-consciousness in Puccha Annapurna's "Pelli" where the protagonist understands the value of her traditions and culture only after moving away from her native land to the alien one. The immigrants speak about distance as a factor that helps them evaluate their Indian roots. The physical and spiritual distance from India is seen necessary to establish an effective connection within and a deeper understanding of Indian values.

We may conclude by saying that cultural identity is a powerful issue for Indians in the United States as reflected in the short stories. The idea of complete assimilation is resisted by the characters. The characters show a strong sense of ethnic identification with their root cultures. There is one final question that remains to be answered. It is whether issues of ethnicity and cultural identity are relevant only to first-generation immigrants, or whether they are relevant to succeeding generations. Answers to these questions can be found only through studies which focus primarily on second- and third-generation immigrants.

NOTES

1. See Desi's *Rooted Homelands* for a more detailed reading of this aspect.
2. My observation is based on Joan's *Asian American Experience*.

Chapter 5

Conclusion

This chapter brings together the themes and trends that emerge in order to understand how Indians of the diaspora migrate and maintain their family, children and religion. This summarizes all my findings in the book that throw light on the works of diasporic women writers. The book has dealt with theories of diaspora, reviewing the sociological aspects of diasporic Indians, linking them with selected literary works of Indian women writers writing in Telugu and English.

Each of these writers in their works contributes to issues of conflict and stress they face as immigrants and strives to create a new identity in the United States. In significant ways, the stories of these writers reflect something of the cold, silent violence inherent in a society that is still reaching out to the future. The writers chosen for this study demonstrate the complexity of the Indian immigrant struggle in the United States.

II

The introduction attempted to assess the causes of migration in general. It also discussed diasporic writings in general and their contribution to Indian English literature. It talked about Telugu writing in America and its influence on succeeding generations. The introduction also states the concept of ethnic identity as an evolving process, rather than a fixed state. It looked at the Indian women writers who script narratives by which future generations of Telugu-Americans and Indian-Americans will live.

These narratives also portray their sacrifice and the struggle they undergo to accommodate to American culture.

It is a difficult thing for the Indian immigrants to balance both the worlds and try to have the best of them. The purpose of this study has been to explore stories written by Telugu diasporic writers and writers writing in English to discover their status in American society with respect to their marital relations, generational gap, and caste and religious and cultural factors. The findings suggest that Indians identify family values, language and religion as the main indicators of their identity. There are a number of factors which influence and have an impact on the formation of their identity. These influences can be divided into three categories:

- Family influences
- Parent-child influences
- Religion and cultural influences.

These factors have been dealt with in detail in three chapters.

The second chapter foregrounded the issue of family influence probing into the lives of the Indian immigrants in America through certain characters in the texts written by diasporic Indian women writers in Telugu and in English. Indians place high value on their peer groups in terms of their family, caste or region. Therefore, much care is taken in the process of choosing a spouse. Parents and relatives, who arrange a marriage, make sure that family, caste and religion remain intact. They also use pressure from the family and other relatives, and sometimes friends, to mediate in case any differences of opinion arise between husband and wife.

Even in the alien land, the struggle for maintaining a strong marital bond is reflected in many of the short stories. Puccha Annapurna in her story "Pelli" (Marriage) exemplifies this view:

> People over here [Americans] are used to this but our people who have immigrated have also started it. How many years have they

> been together? Without any reason men and women are opting for divorce. (103)

Most of the stories portray the adjustment in the marital relationships while the others talk about the advantages of being away from homeland to lead an independent life with less association of the elders. Runu in "Ultra Sound" by Chitra Banerjee Divakaruni is satisfied with the relationship with her husband and feels that she has a voice in decision making:

> I feel additionally fortunate because in Sunil I've found a friend, someone to discuss the perplexities of America with someone who understands. (213)

During many of the interviews with Indian immigrants, I learnt that the husbands and wives, unlike American couples, were not physically close in the open. When questioned about this, one man said, "The couple doesn't hug, or even shake hands. Husbands and wives do not show physical affection for each other in public." Chitra Banerjee Divakaruni's "Clothes" portrays that the husband and wife are not free to express their love in private either:

> I'm breathless with suppressed laughter (Father and Mother Sen must not hear us) and my cheeks are hot with the delicious excitement of conspiracy. We've stuffed a towel at the bottom of the door so no light will shine through. (24-25)

Both the writers in Telugu and English have expressed their views with regard to their idea of marital relationship. In most of the works written by Telugu writers the wife is submissive and obedient to her husband but some stories in English portray women who barge out of the relationships bravely to face the world independently.

"Burning Turtles" by Hema Nair in Sunaina Maira and Rajini Srikanth's *Contours of the Heart* talks about an Indian woman who leads self-determining life with her daughter in the United States. Hema Nair uses the imagery of the turtles that storm out of their shells unable to bear the heat on their hard shell. It can be compared to Indian women in general, who migrate to the Unites States. They build a cocoon around themselves to avoid the fast culture and like turtles they creep back into their shells. But at times, the burning effect of the American culture and its discrimination compel them to come out into the open society to face the consequences. The incident of turtles drives away the fear from our protagonist, and motivates her to come out in the open to face problems in her life, thus contradicting the statement "Indian women are timid." The last sentence, "She would navigate herself home." (347),· portrays her confidence in continuing her future fearlessly to face any obstacles, all by herself.

America represents all that is hoped for under the umbrella of freedom. Most immigrants take it as an advantage while some view it as a demerit. This is what the third chapter deals with. We find that there is the "first generation" of uprooted immigrants drawn to the American fantasy but ill-adapted in language, values and cultural practices. Their hopes lie in the second generation, on the children who master the language and the ways of the new society. But most of these children make their adaptation at the cost of rejecting their parents' way of life, or at least by subordinating it to the new values they imbibe. As Radhika Nori says in "Poriginti Pullakura":

> My hope to at least raise our baby according to our traditions has also become a despair. . . . Does she remember Telugu at all? Even when we speak to her in Telugu, she responds in English . . . the fear haunts me about hearing some bad news of her wrong steps in life. (37)

The major conflict for parents here is with their children than with themselves, i.e., they expect their children to hold on to their culture. On the other hand, these parents do not wish to be so rigid as to cause stress to their offspring. They do not want them to become totally Americanized either. It is well portrayed in the fear of a father towards his daughter in Bharati Mukherjee's short story, "A Father" in *Darkness*.

> He pictured his grandson crawling to him, and the grandson was always fat and buttery-skinned, like the infant Krishna. An American son-in-law was a terrifying notion. (70)

This brings out the cultural conflicts of the immigrants in America. The father is ready to accept a grandson from an unmarried daughter of his but wishes the father to be an Indian.

The third chapter tries to prove that conflicts occur while people try to balance between American society and Indian values. There is a general progression in the identity conflicts for the parents. They immigrate of their own choice and are well-equipped with their past traditions and culture. They also try to adapt to the new one, while involving their children in Indian culture and tradition. The children tend to develop new meanings for the symbols of their culture, not quite understanding them in the same way as their parents. Soma Sudeshana Reddy's "Mogudu Kaavala" reflects this turmoil of Seema, a second-generation immigrant:

> Desires, traditions, culture, sorrows and the instinct to differentiate between man and woman, all these she tried to instill in Seema . . . so much of anguish and care for me and my future. . . . She wailed. (157)

Writers who write in Telugu differ from writers in English as they have an additional bond they wish to keep intact to their language. The characters in the Telugu stories tend to develop dual identities, one as a Telugu in American society and the other as an Indian in the American culture. Here mothers often appear more insistent in the maintenance of Telugu language and culture at home.

For most immigrants, Indian culture is what is lived at home, while the American counterpart is what is lived at work. Thus, the fourth chapter deals with Gregory Lee Petty's views of America as the land of unbridled individualism, of lack of self-discipline or a sense of family obligation and duty. On the other hand maintaining one's Indian identity has its risks, as it may lead to one in becoming marginalized in the American society.

There seems to be a feeling on the part of the Telugu immigrants to move towards regional, caste and family identity. This is particularly true as the number of Telugus and members from each caste increase. Immigrants, out of a nostalgic yearning for the traditional heritage strive to recapture their cultural tradition. For them, Indian culture acts as the background against which American culture is analyzed and understood. The two cultures act on them to make them feel confused and out-of-place; they are reminded sometimes that they do not quite fit in either world. Chimata Kamala in "America Illaalu" portrays the above in a normal Indian woman when she migrates to the United States:

> I came here an innocent dressed in a silk saree, marigold decked in my hair, with bright beautiful ear-rings hanging, looked like a doll of Krishna Sastry, a typical village girl, like a traditional Indian wife. I noticed many changes along with time. Lot of adjustments took place not only in my attire but also in my culture. (78)

A clear indication of the culture-crossing is manifested in Bharati Mukherjee's short stories. The author shows a considerable degree of this crossing and the irony in trying to separate the traditional one from the westernized characters in her fiction. In the case of writers living in the west, one sees the alienation quite clearly, because they feel that theirs is a broken fragmented identity. This is brought out in the "Hindus" in Mukherjee's *Darkness*:

> An Indian woman is brought up to please. No matter how passionately we link bodies with our new countries, we never escape the early days. . . . No matter what language I speak it will come out slightly foreign, no matter how perfectly I mouth it. (139-40)

Indian immigrants do not write from the position of a distinct foreign community, but their writings reflect the perspective of someone caught between two cultures. They may look back on India with nostalgia, asserting their biculturalism, but they also look on their new land as outsiders with a feeling of something that they have lost.

Religion and caste also play a vital role in sustaining Indian culture in an alien land. Almost all the writers that I have dealt with are from the upper class, upper caste background. Their stories therefore give importance to their religion and caste backgrounds. Though there is a reference to caste, even if it be about the upper-caste, with reference to Telugu writers, this is totally absent in writers writing in English.

Here I would like to talk about Meena Alexander, a Christian writer in the West who has not explicitly dealt with the concept of religion as the other writers have done. My personal interaction with her reminds me of her statement that she was looked down upon as an Indian by the westerners who have termed her to be a Hindu because she is an Indian. As a Christian, Hindu pujas and rituals have never been a part of her so as to complicate her identity. Thus we find the absence of religion in her works. In her novel *Manhattan Music*, she says:

> failure to provide any support and certitude from pain, Sandhya breaks down and tries to kill herself with a rope around her neck in her friend Draupadi's flat. (223)

She uses traditional Hindu names for her characters, e.g. Draupadi, a tough and resilient woman like her namesake in the *Mahabharata*. Meena Alexander's works are given importance and are popular. We notice that her identity in terms of caste and religion are not significant in her being viewed as an author. However the establishment of different Telugu associations on the basis of caste proves the above argument that non-Hindu Telugu writers are neglected.

There is a difference in the writers writing in Telugu, where not a single writer from the lower class and lower caste background is found in any of the published books or journals. There are instances when I met non-Hindu and lower caste women writers and came to know that their articles, poems and fiction have never been accepted by publishing houses.

The absence of published material by such writers in Telugu forced me to confine my study to women writers from upper caste, upper class backgrounds. The selected writers and works are representative of the other writers in the diaspora. Similarly, lack of second-generation writers in Telugu has forced me to concentrate on the first-generation writers. There are second-generation women writers from Telugu background who write in English. Here we can see the influence of the colonial language on them while their parents struggle to write in Telugu to preserve the language and to pass it on to future generations.

At this stage I would like to talk about Jhumpa Lahiri, writing in English, who has a Bengali background. I have already referred to her work in the introduction. Here I would like to discuss her book *Interpreter of Maladies: Stories from Bengal, Boston and Beyond*. It bagged the Pulitzer Prize for fiction in 2000. It is a great honour for an Indian writer writing in English. It is a great milestone after Arundhati Roy's *The God of Small Things*. Interestingly, the nine stories from Lahiri's book talk about the very issues I deal with in the three chapters that I have discussed—marital relationships, first- and second generation conflicts, religion and culture.

Jhumpa Lahiri's stories reveal what she has achieved in her maiden venture. There is no sequential development of the stories. She has evolved her own style in dealing with such sensitive issues by changing the mode of narration from past to the present and again reversing it without being nostalgic. Almost all stories end on a positive note, with the hope of a "tomorrow" which suggests that with little effort we can discard our cultural problems and move towards a society where the traditional and the modern would meet in the inherent goodness, asserting the worth of human life.

III

Having discussed all the issues that propped up in the short stories, I find that America is viewed as a magnet by the Indian immigrants. It is regarded as a land of dedicated and hardworking citizens and a country of producers. For them living in both the worlds not only means facing the best of both worlds, but also the worst of both. Being "too" Indian and "too" American is a disadvantage for them. An attempt is made therefore in this book to get a glimpse of their diversity by studying Telugu women writers along with women writers writing in English.

Indians are a diverse population with multiple cultures and customs co-existing simultaneously. No single project can adequately capture "the Asian Indian identity." An attempt has been made therefore in this book to get a glimpse of this diversity by studying Telugu women writers along with some women writers writing in English. Telugus are one of the many sub-groups in the United States that are struggling to develop their own language and culture. This book shows the values the Telugus wish to restore in terms of their culture, tradition and literature. The works of the diasporic Telugu writers provide us with an opportunity to view the Telugu families, the conflicts and struggles they undergo in maintaining their identity. The study of their literature confirms the important role they accord to the family in supporting and influencing the formation of their identity.

Stories in English show that ignoring the family will greatly undermine a valuable part of the diasporic Indian. In spite of over-generalizations, these stories are narratives that portray the fear of the immigrant characters in a new world. Some characters find their fears confirmed while others are pleasantly surprised. The works of the diasporic writers both in Telugu and English make it clear that it is always better for the immigrants not to forget their roots. Rather they can have the "best" of both the worlds. The research also emphasizes the need to take into consideration factors like caste, region, religion and culture in the formation of the identity of the Indian diaspora.

As family plays a vital role in the identity formation, so too do religion and culture. In almost all the stories, religion has been the main basis for their ethnic identity. In stories written in Telugu and English, the main differences in attitudes are linked to religion and social class. This study suggests that they have a lot to live up to in maintaining their culture and identity.

Therefore I view the whole experience in terms of America being the chosen land and immigrants in "Trishanku Swargam."

This study has also outlined an emerging genre of stories by Telugu immigrants which will shape and influence future generations of writers as well as future immigrants, to inform them what it means to be a Telugu American and an Indian American. The study is particularly important for those immigrants who come without the resources and skills that these present groups of immigrants possess. The writers also feel that their parents have, on the whole, tolerated prejudice, discrimination and harassment, perhaps at the price of settling in America. But the second generation is not prepared to accept this. Overall, the approach of young Indians seems to be for continuity and change, sometimes leading to tensions between generations. In brief, second-generation Indians are adopting a new culture which is a synthesis of the "old" and the "new."

The findings of this project may aid future researchers in identifying areas of conflict and resolution with regard to the Indian diasporic literature in America. This project may provide the springboard for more research on how Telugus in particular and Indians in general maintain their identity in the United States. Further research needs to be done which explores the second generation. As my study is perhaps the first of its kind to use Telugu writing, I hope it will trigger off more comparative and interdisciplinary studies involving other regional languages in India.

For me women writers can be read in isolation, but I did not follow any single approach to defend this statement for there is no apparent feministic approach in this study. I talked about both the merits and demerits of being a wife, mother and woman in the American society. I did not dare to compare them with male writers because they would not have as much emotion and not have been as explicit as the women writers. Especially while dealing with motherhood, women writers look at its complexities. Given the fact that I have taken my subject to be a woman, I feel that it is essential to study these works from the perspective of a male researcher for purposes of comparison. Studying and comparing male writers may enrich our understanding of the Indian diaspora.

Bibliography

Agarwal, Priya. *Passage from India's Post-1965 Indian Immigrants and their Children: Conflicts, Concerns, and Solutions*. Palos Verdes: Yuvathi, 1991.

Agnew, Vijay, ed. *Diaspora, Memory and Identity: A Search for Home*. Toronto: Toronto UP, 2005.

Ahmed, Ali Jimale. *Diaspora Blues*. Trenton: Red Sea, 2005.

Ahmed, Yasmin. *Gendering the Diaspora: Continuity and Development in Post-War Asian British Women's Writing*. London: London UP, 2005.

Alexander Meena. *The Bird's Bright Ring: A Long Poem*. Calcutta: Writers Workshop, 1976.

______. *House of a Thousand Doors: Poems and Prose Pieces*. Washington D.C.: Three Continents, 1988.

______. *I Root My Name*. Calcutta: United Writers, 1977.

______. *Manhattan Music*. San Francisco: Mercury, 1997.

______. *Nampally Road*. San Francisco: Mercury, 1991.

______. *Night-Scene, the Garden*. New York: Red Dust, 1992.

______. *Stone Roots*. New Delhi: Arnold-Heinemann, 1980.

______. *The Storm: A Poem in Five Parts*. New York: Red Ducat, 1989.

______. *Without Place*. Calcutta: Writers Workshop, 1978.

Ali, Suki. *Mixed-Race, Post-Race: Gender, New Ethnicities and Cultural Practices*. Oxford: Berg, 2003.

Anderson, Wanni W. and Robert G. Lee, ed. *Displacements and Diasporas: Asians in the Americas*. New Brunswick: Rutgers UP, 2005.

Annapurna, Puccha. "Pelli." Sarma and Bala 101-13.

Anwar, Muhammad. *Between Cultures: Continuity and Change in the Lives of Young Asians*. London: Routledge, 1998.

Assayag, Jackie and Veronique Benei, ed. *At Home in Diaspora: South Asian Scholars and the West*. Bloomington: Indiana UP, 2003.

Bande, Usha. *Cultural Space and Diaspora: Journey Metaphor in Indian Women's Writing*. Shimla: Indian Institute of Advanced Study, 2003.

Bates, Crispin, ed. *Community, Empire and Migration: South Asians in Diaspora*. New York: Palgrave, 2001.

Bhachu, Parminder. *Dangerous Designs: Asian Women Fashion, the Diaspora Economies*. New York: Routledge, 2004.

Bhagavati. "Maa Vidakulu Maavidakulu." *Telugu Varadhi*. New York: ATA, 1992.

Bhatt, Yashoda and Yamuna Rajarao, ed. *The Image of Woman in Indian Literature*. Delhi: B.R, 1993.

Blunt, Alison. *Domicile and Diaspora: Anglo-Indian Women and Spatial Politics of Home*. Malden: Blackwell, 2005.

Bracks, Lean'tin L. *Writings on Black Women of the Diaspora: History, Language and Identity*. New York: Garland, 1998.

Braziel, Jana Evens, ed. *Theorizing Diaspora: A Reader*. Malden: Blackwell, 2003.

Brenner, Frederic. *Diaspora: Homelands in Exile*. New York: Harper Collins, 2003.

Bromely, Roger. *Narratives for a New Belonging: Diasporic Cultural Fictions*. Edinburgh: Edinburgh UP, 2000.

Brown, Wesley and Ling Amy, ed. *Imagining America: Short Stories—An Anthology of American Fiction*. New Delhi: UBS, 1995.

Carter, Marina and Khal Torabully, ed. *Coolitude: An Anthology of the Indian Labour Diaspora*. London: Anthem, 2002.

Chamberlain, Mary. *Family Love in the Diaspora: Migration and the Anglo-Caribbean Experience*. New Brunswick: Transaction, 2006.

Chand, Neerja. "An Aesthetic of Dislocation." Dhawan 141-51.

Clammer, John. *Diaspora and Identity: The Sociology of Culture in South East Asia*. Jalen: Pelanduk, 2002.

Collier, Mary Jane, ed. *Intercultural Alliances: Critical Transformation*. Thousand Oaks: Sage, 2003.

Crane, Ralph J. and Radhika Mohan Ram, ed. *Shifting Continents/ Colliding Cultures: Diaspora Writing of the Indian Sub-Continent*. Amsterdam: Rodopi, 2000.

Dasgupta, Sati S. *On the Trial of an Uncertain Dream: Indian Immigrant Experience in America*. New York: AMS, 1989.

Dass, Veena Noble, ed. *Feminism and Literature*. New Delhi: Prestige, 1995.

De, Shobha. *Socialite Evenings*. New Delhi: Penguin, 1988.

Deshpande, Shashi. *Roots and Shadows*. Bombay: Sangam, 1983.

Desi, Jigna. *Rooted Homelands, Routed Host lands: (En)Gendered Mobility in the South Asian Diaspora*. Ann Arbor: Bell, 1999.

Dhawan, R.K, ed. *Writers of the Indian Diaspora*. New Delhi: Prestige, 2001.

Divakaruni, Chitra Banerjee. *Arranged Marriage*. London: Black Swan-Transworld, 1997.

_____. *Black Candle: Poems about Women from India, Pakistan and Bangladesh*. Corvallis: Calyx, 1991.

_____. "We the Indian Women in America." Maira and Srikanth 268-270.

Dubey, Ajay, ed. *Indian Diaspora: Global Identity*. Delhi: Kalinga, 2003.

Durga, Kanaka. "Henpecked." Venugopalarao, vol. 7. 90-98.

Fisher, Maxine P. *The Indians of New York City: A Study of Immigrants from India*. New Delhi: Heritage, 1980.

Ghosh, Lipi and Ramkrishna Chatterjee, ed. *Indian Diaspora in Asian and Pacific Regions: Culture, People and Interactions*. Jaipur: Rawat, 2004.

Gourdine, Angelleta K.M. *The Difference Place Makes: Gender, Sexuality and Diaspora Identity*. Columbus: Ohio UP, 2002.

Gregory, James N. *The Southern Diaspora: How the Great Migrations of Black and White Southerners Transformed America*. Chapel Hill: North Carolina UP, 2005.

Gupta, Himanee. *American Places, Indian Spaces: Post-1965 Immigrants Negotiate Self and Community*. Ann Arbor: Bell, 2000.

Haar, Gerrie Ter, ed. *Religious Communities in the Diaspora*. Nairobi: Acton, 2001.

Hall, Stuart. "Cultural Identity and Representation." Rutherford 221-25

Hollywood Bollywood. Deepa Mehta. David Hamilton, 2002.

The Holy Bible. Kings James Version. London: Cambridge UP, 2001.

Huang, Shirlena, Peggy Teo and S. Brenda, A. Yeoh, ed. *Diasporic Subjects and Identity Negotiations: Women in and from Asia*. Oxford: Pergamon, 2000.

Hussain, Yasmin. *Writing Diaspora: South Asian Women, Culture and Ethnicity*. Aldershot: Ashgate, 2005.

Jacobsen, Knut A. and P. Pratap Kumar, ed. *South Asians in the Diaspora: Histories and Religious Traditions*. Boston: Brill, 2004.

Jagat K. Motwani, Mahin Gosine and Jyoti Barot-Motwani, ed. *Global Indian Diaspora: Yesterday, Today and Tomorrow*. New York: GOPIO, 1993.

Jain, Jasbir, ed. *Writers of the Indian Diaspora: Theory and Practice*. Jaipur: Rawat, 1998.

Jain, Prakash C. *Racial Discrimination against Overseas Indians: A Class Analysis*. New Delhi: Concept, 1990.

Jain, R. *Family Violence in India*. New Delhi: Radiant, 1992.

Jayaram, N, ed. *Indian Diaspora: Dynamics of Migration*. New Delhi: Sage, 2004.

Joan, Faung Jean Lee. *Asia American Experiences in the United States.* London: McFarland, 1999.

Jonnal, Lalitha. "Abhaagyathudu." Venugopalarao, vol. 7. 79-89.

Kamala, Chimata. "America Illaalu." Sarma and Bala. 76-79.

_____. *America Illaalu.* Stafford: Vanguri Foundation, 2000.

_____. "Namarupaalu." Kamala 50-53.

Kelly, Jennifer. *Borrowed Identities.* New York: P. Lang, 2004.

Kimeera, Yarlagadda. "Veedina Needalu." Sarma and Bala, 212-17.

Koslowski, Rey, ed. *International Migration and the Globalisation of Domestic Politics.* London: Routledge, 2005.

Kurian, George and Ram P Srivastava. *Overseas Indians: A Study in Adaptation.* New Delhi: Vikas, 1983.

Laguerre, Michel S. *Diasporic Citizenship: Haitian Americans in Transnational America.* Basingstoke: Macmillan, 1998.

_____. *Urban Multiculturalism and Globalisation in New York City: An Analysis of Diasporic Temporalities.* Basingstoke: Macmillan, 2003.

Lahiri, Jhumpa. *Interpreter of Maladies: Stories of Bengal, Boston and Beyond.* New Delhi: Harper Collins, 1999.

Levy, Andre and Alex Weingrod, ed. *Homelands and Diasporas: Holy Lands and Other Places.* Stanford: Stanford UP, 2005.

Lim, Shirley and Amy Ling, ed. *Reading the Literatures of Asian American.* Philadelphia: Temple UP, 1992.

Mahajan, Amarjit and Madhurima. *Family Violence and Abuse in India.* New Delhi: Deep, 1995.

Mahalakshmi, Pattisapu Radha. "Smoky Mountains." Venugopalarao. vol. 7. 59-70.

Maira, Sunaina and Rajini Srikanth, ed. *Contours of the Heart.* Philadelphia: Temple UP, 1998.

Mandal, Somdatta, ed. *Asian American Writing: The Diasporic Imagination.* New Delhi: Prestige, 2000.

Manian, Padam. *Straddling Two Cultures: Asian Indian Children in America.* San Francisco: Many Cultures, 1997.

Markandaya, Kamala. *Nectar in a Sieve.* Bombay: Jaico, 1955.

Mcleod, A.L., ed. *The Literature of Indian Diaspora: Essays in Criticism.* New Delhi: Sterling, 2000.

Meer, Ameena. "I Want to Give You Devotion." Maira and Srikanth, 92-106.

Mehta, Brinda J. *Diasporic (Dis)locations: Indo-Caribbean Women Writers Negotiate the Kala Pani.* Kingston: West Indies UP, 2004.

Mishra, Pramod and Urmila Mohapatra, ed. *South Asian Diaspora in North America: An Annotated Bibliography.* Delhi: Kalinga, 2002.

Mitra, Anuradha M. "Romantic Stereotypes." Maira and Srikanth, 421-29.

Modi, Ishwar, ed. *Emerging Trends in Indian Sociology*. Jaipur: Rawat, 1986.

Mortland,Carol A., ed. *Diasporic Identity*. Arlington: America Anthropological Association, 1998.

Mukherjee, Bharati. *Darkness*. Penguin: New Delhi, 1990.

_____. *Middleman and Other Stories*. Penguin: New Delhi, 1991.

Mukhi, Sunita Sunder. *Doing the Desi thing: Performing Indianness in New York City*. New York: Garland, 2000.

Murthy, Kavita. *Intergenerational Comparisons of Perceptions of Love and Marriage among Asian Indians: A Qualitative Inquiry*. Ann Arbor: Bell, 1997.

Nair, Hema. "Burning Turtles." Maira and Srikanth, 332-49.

Nasta, Susheila. *Home Truths: Fictions of the South Asian Diaspora in Britain*. New York: Palgrave, 2002.

Nelson, Emmanuel S., ed. *Reworlding: The Literature of the Indian Diaspora*. Westport: Greenwood, 1992.

_____, ed. *Writers of the Indian Diaspora: A Bio-Bibliographical Sourcebook*. Westport: Greenwood, 1993.

Ng, Franklin, ed. *Asians in America: The Peoples of East, South East, and South Asia in American Life and Culture*. New York: Garland, 1998.

Nori, Radhika. "Poriginti Pullakura." Sarma and Bala, 36-40.

Pal, Adesh, ed. *Interpreting Indian Diasporic Experience*. New Delhi: Creative, 2004.

Parekh, Bhikhu, Gurharpat Singh and Steven Vertovec, ed. *Culture and Economy in the Indian Diaspora*. London: Routledge, 2003.

Petievich, Carla, ed. *The Expanding Landscape: South Asians and the Diaspora*. New Delhi: Manohar, 1999.

Pettys, Gregory Lee. *Asian Indians in the United States: An Analysis of Identity Formation and Retention*. Ann Arbor: Bell, 1997.

Ponzanesi, Sandra. *Paradoxes of Postcolonial Culture: Contemporary Women Writers of the Indian and Afro-Italian Diaspora*. Albany: New York UP, 2004.

Puwar, Nirmal and Parvati Raghuram, ed. *South Asian Women in the Diaspora*. New York: Berg, 2003.

Radhakrishnan, R. *Diasporic Mediations: Between Home and Location*. Minneapolis: Minneapolis UP, 1996.

Rajan, Gita and Sailaja Sharma, ed. *New Cosmopolitanisms: South Asians in the U.S.* Stanford: Stanford UP, 2006.

Rangaswamy, Padma. *Namaste America: Indian Immigrants in an American Metropolis*. University Park: Pennsylvania UP, 2000.

Ravindra, K. Jain. *Indian Communities Abroad: Themes and Literature*. New Delhi: Manohar, 1993.

Rayaprol, Aparna. *Negotiating Identities: Women in the Diaspora*. New York: Oxford UP, 1997.

Reddy, Soma Sudeshana. "Chaitanyam." Venugopalarao, vol. 6. 77-94.

_____. "Passing Phase." *Proceedings of Fourth International Telugu Conference*. New York: ATA, 1992. 129-31.

Ruether, Rosemary Radford, ed. *Gender Ethnicity and Religion: Views from the Other Side*. Minneapolis: Fortress, 2002.

Russell, Elizabeth, ed. *Caught between Cultures: Women, Writing and Subjectivities*. Amsterdam: Rodopi, 2002.

Rutherford J., ed. *Identity: Community, Culture, Difference*. London: Lawrence, 1990.

Saran, Paramatma and Edwin Eames, ed. *The New Ethnics: Asian Indians in the United States*. New York: Praeger, 1980.

Saran, Paramatma. *The Asian Indian Experience in the United States*. Cambridge: Schenkman, 1985.

Sarma, Indraganti Srikantha and Indraganti Janaki Bala, ed. *America Telugu Katha*. Houston: Vanguri Foundation, 2002.

Sarma, Pudipedhi Seshu. "Aasakiranam." Venugopalarao. vol. 5. 16-20.

_____. "Abhaasulu—Abhaathulu." Venugopalarao. vol. 7. 8-13.

_____."Agaadham." Venugopalarao, vol. 3. 5-10.

_____. "Pelli Chesukunte Chudu." Venugopalarao. vol. 8. 35-39.

_____. "Sangarshana," "Surprise." Venugopalarao. vol. 4. 52-56 and 89-95.

Sen, Ruma Jhuma. *Articulating Identity at the Interstices of Home, Nation, Race, and Gender: A Critical Ethnography of New Asian Indian immigrant Experiences*. Ann Arbor: Bell, 2002.

Sethi, S. Prakash. *The New Assimilative Immigrants: An Opinion-Attitude Survey of Asian Indian Influential in the United States*. New York: Baruch, 1988.

Shani, Giorgiandrea. *Globalisation and Identity: Sikh Nationalism, Diaspora and International Relations*. London: London UP, 2005.

Shankar, Lavina Dhingra and Rajini Srikanth, ed. *A Part Yet Apart*. Philadelphia: Temple UP, 1998.

Sharma, Kavita A., Adeṣh Pal and Tapas Chakrabarti, ed. *Theorizing and Critiquing Indian Diaspora*. New Delhi: Creative, 2004.

Sharma, Rekha and E. Annamalai, ed. *Indian Diaspora: In Search of Identity*. Mysore: CIIL, 2003.

Shukla, Sandhya Rajendra. *India Abroad: Diasporic Cultures of Post-War America and England*. Princeton: Princeton UP, 2003.

Sicakkan, Hakan G and Yngve G. Lithman, ed. *What Happens When a Society is Diverse: Exploring Multidimensional Identities*. New York: Edwin Mellen, 2006.

Singh, Daman and Mahavir Singh, ed. *Indians Abroad*. Haryana: Hope India, 2003.

Singh, Hardayal. *"Being Indian in Jersey City": Asian American Experience in the United States*. London: Mcfarland, 1991.

Stout, Daniel A. and Judith M. Buddenbaum, ed. *Religion and Popular Culture: Studies on the Interaction of World Views*. Iowa: Iowa UP, 2001.

Stuart, Cunningham and John Sinclair, ed. *Floating Lives: The Media and Asian Diasporas*. Lanham: Rowman, 2001.

Turino, Thomas. *Identity and the Arts in Diaspora Communities*. Warren: Harmonie, 2004.

Uma, Alladi. *Woman and her Family: Indian and Afro-American—A Literary Perspective*. New Delhi: Sterling, 1989.

Varma, Sushma J. and Radhika Seshan. ed. *Fractured Identity: The Indian Diaspora in Canada*. New Delhi: Rawat, 2003.

Veeramaneni, Giridhar. *Enjoy the Journey*. Toronto: Dev, 2004.

Venugopal, C.N. *Religion and Indian Society: A Sociological Perspective*. New Delhi: Gyan, 1998.

Venugopalarao, Pemmaraju, ed. *America Telugu Kathanika*. 8 vols. Houston: Vanguri Foundation, 1995-2004.

Volga. *Rajakeeya Kathalu*. Hyderabad: Visalandra, 1997.

_____. "Badhratha." Volga 35-39.

Waller, Marguerite R. and Sylvia Marcos, ed. *Dialogue and Difference: Feminisms Challenge Globalisation*. New York: Palgrave, 2005.

Wanni, W. Anderson and Robert G. Lee. *Displacements and Diasporas: Asians in the Americas*. New Brunswick: Rutgers UP, 2005.

Warner R. Stephen, ed. *Gatherings in Diaspora: Religious Communities and the New Immigration*. Philadelphia: Temple UP, 1998.

West, Russell. *Transcultural Graffiti: Diasporic Writing and the Teaching of Literary Studies*. Amsterdam: Rodopi, 2005.

Williams, Raymond B. *Religions of Immigrants from India and Pakistan New Threads in the American Tapestry*. Cambridge: Cambridge UP, 1998.